MW01634400

THE 11 SECRETS OF HIGHLY INFLUENTIAL IT LEADERS

The critical path to accessing and succeeding in the executive suite

Marc J. Schiller

Reprint Requests
Rain Partners, LLC
875 Mamaroneck Avenue - Suite 304
Mamaroneck, NY 10528

First edition
Published by Rain Partners, LLC
Designed by Dalma Design, Inc. New York, NY

ISBN 978-0-615-43628-9

CONTENTS

FOREWORD

Before you get started on The Journey

There are a few things that you should know.

My primary goal in this book is to reach out to IT leaders—today's and tomorrow's. Although many of the stories and lessons reference the CIO, *The Secrets* apply equally to IT managers still working their way into the upper echelons of IT management. In fact, the earlier you learn *The Secrets* the better.

Much of this book deals with the relationship between the IT leader and his/her colleagues within the organization in which they work. Since the vast majority of my experience has been in the commercial world, I often refer to this organization as "the business." However, from the experience I have had with non-profits, I have yet to find any meaningful differences in the organizational dynamics as it relates to the role of the IT leader. As such, although I may use the term "business," everything in this book applies equally to not-for-profit organizations.

Unfortunately, the majority of the stories in this book refer to male CIOs. There are however a couple of wonderful exceptions. And while more women are slowly making their way into the senior ranks of IT management, it has not traditionally been an area that has drawn a lot of women. That's unfortunate, because as a general rule, I have found the women IT managers with whom I have worked to be particularly strong, and I look forward to seeing more women in IT leadership roles. I believe the profession will benefit greatly from it. In the meantime, please forgive the overuse of the male pronoun. It reflects an imperfect reality, not a personal bias.

In comparison to most books on IT management and leadership, this book is "small." This was done very much by design and was the product of hard work. As you will shortly see, a key theme of this book is debunking conventional wisdom as it relates to IT management practices. Conventional books on IT management often contain pages and pages of confusing diagrams, frameworks and so-called methodologies; the value and use of which is pretty dubious in most cases. You'll find none of that in the pages to come. No complex drawings with stacks, pyramids and arrows galore accompanied by long-winded explanations. Just what I hope you will find to be crisp and highly useful insights.

Stories

Nearly everything contained within this book is in some way attributable to what I have learned from other people. In some cases, particularly when I use case studies and real-life stories, it's easy to credit the appropriate people and I delight in doing so by directly naming them and their companies at the time. In the cases where I am unable to use real names, I instead use a changed first name followed by a changed last initial. Any similarity between my chosen names and any real people with the same first names and last initials is purely coincidental.

Citations

This book is not, however, only a collection of stories. In addition to my personal experiences, a great deal of research was undertaken to support the publication of this book. The research spans numerous primary and secondary sources. In an effort to provide proper attribution without cluttering the text with a complex set of qualifying footnotes, I have employed the following citation practice: At the end of the book I provide a comprehensive list of references. It contains a list of all the books, articles, studies, essays, blogs and websites mentioned, or in any way consulted, as part of writing this book. Accordingly, when you encounter the mention of any article, book or survey in the body of the book, you can be sure to find it in the references section.

Finally, direct quotes obtained during the course of my years working with clients or via primary research are fully attributed in the body of the book as are any surveys or other primary research materials mentioned herein.

Acknowledgements

My deepest thanks and gratitude to the many people who have made this book possible. First and foremost to my clients, colleagues and industry friends across the world. Without you, there would be no stories to tell, no lessons to teach.

There are however a few people who require special mention and thanks. To my incredible sister Carol, for helping with everything from concept vetting, drafting, editing and so much more. To Christopher Gorgoni, for suffering through the endless refinement of ideas with me until it was just right. To Linda Rosencrance for the many long-distance writing and editing calls. To Carmen Silano for printing out yet another draft of secret number whatever. To Roy Speed for your help and friendship at a critical time. But even more, for the tools and many brilliant lessons on what writing is all about. To David Azran for yet another terrific design. To the wonderful people and place of Steamboat Springs, Colorado where much of this book was conceived and written in the shadows of your snow-covered mountains. And most of all, to my wife Karyn and our two daughters Yael and Gabriella for encouraging me in your uniquely humorous ways.

The Journey | THE MAN FROM MARS AND IT LEADERS

Shortly after the "pooper scooper" laws were passed in New York City, a late-night comedian noted that, "if a man from Mars came to earth and saw how we walk our dogs and pick up after them, he would naturally approach the dog and say, take me to your leader."

It's a funny joke. And it works because it exposes an incongruity—an irony of sorts. Here we are, supposedly the "superior" human race, and yet we are the ones picking up the dog's poop.

I like the man from Mars test. It's a quick and easy way to analyze a situation with a basic question: Does this make sense? If a man from Mars came down and looked at this situation, would it make sense to him? When the answer is "no, it wouldn't," then I know, despite all the explanations in the world, that there is probably something wrong in the situation. The incongruity expressed by the man from Mars test points to something bigger at play. (That, or we have another good late-night joke.)

This brings me to the basic question that underlies this book: If a man from Mars came down with a mission to report back on the state of IT leaders on planet Earth, people like you and me, what would he say about us and about our professional lives?

After browsing hundreds (maybe even thousands) of professional websites, magazines, journals, blogs, podcasts and YouTube channels, and then perusing the agendas and abstracts of a few dozen industry conferences that touch on issues of IT leadership and management, his report would probably sound something like this:

" IT leaders (sometimes called IT managers, directors or CIOs) are under assault. Everywhere I look I see articles and stories about the serious problems they face. Undermined by their peers at every turn, their value and contribution constantly questioned by their superiors, they are in perpetual search of "alignment" with the stakeholders they serve in the hope it will save their job from the dreaded outsourcing trend.

Leading academics and researchers in the field publicly declare that "IT no longer matters," and they are counseled by journalists to develop all manner of business and relationship skills to avoid extinction. It is of little surprise that so many of them report such a low level of satisfaction with their careers today and their prospects for tomorrow.

Still, they are a brave group. They fight on in search of answers to their existential questions—questions like:

- What to do for their opinions to be respected and valued by their colleagues?

- How to be invited to participate in key decision making forums and contribute to their organization's strategy?

- Is there a path that leads to the senior leadership ranks of their organization?

In light of the above, I suggest we avoid getting too close to this group, lest we be labeled "geek lovers." I fear it could negatively impact our relationship with the rest of human society on earth."

It's not really that bad, is it?

That's what you're probably thinking right now. It's not really that bad, is it? I know, it's hard to believe; but it's the truth. At least that's the story we keep telling ourselves.

If you're going to take the man from Mars test, you have to be willing to see things with unbiased eyes. And unfortunately, I think that's exactly how a man from Mars would see things, because there is lots of data to support this view.

A quick review of what's being written about in leading IT leadership and management publications reveals what's top of mind for today's IT leaders:

- Do CIOs Still Matter?
- Why CFOs and CEOs Hate IT
- Proving IT's Value to the Business
- IT Leadership: Building a Business Case to Save Your Job
- Battling Lack of IT Understanding
- How to Communicate ROI to the Business
- IT Does So Matter
- Why CIOs are Last Among Equals

These items appear in leading publications because they reflect the issues and concerns of IT leaders. Clearly, something is going on.

It's not just the media

It's not just journalists and industry commentators who point to these issues. CIO peer groups, technology industry associations and other professional groups present a similar picture of pain and suffering but with the additional credibility of an insider.

Take for example the CIO Executive Council, a peer group of over 500 CIOs. They conduct a variety of programs and meetings geared to serve the needs of their members. During 2010 the council identified a number of built-in challenges or paradoxes inherent in the role of today's CIO. These paradoxes then became agenda items for council meetings across the country. Let's look at a few of them:

- "You were hired to be strategic but you are forced to spend most of your time on operational issues"

- "Your many successes are invisible; your few mistakes are highly visible"

- "IT can make or break a company, but you are not a member of the corporate board"

- "You run one of the most pervasive, critical functions, yet you must prove your value constantly"

- "You are intimately involved in every facet of the business, yet you are considered separate and apart from it"

These paradoxes may indeed exist for many in IT. But if you look carefully at them, you can also see that they express a feeling, a desire for a different reality and less of an objective truth.

With that in mind, take a second look at these "paradoxes" along with my translation of them—gleaned from dozens of interviews with, and hundreds of survey responses from, IT leaders. This translation illustrates beautifully (and painfully) how IT leaders really feel about their roles.

CIO Council Paradox	Translation
"You were hired to be strategic but you are forced to spend most of your time on operational issues."	Many IT leaders like to think they were hired to be engaged in strategy (usually not the case). They feel frustrated at not being invited into strategy forums and blame operational necessities for their absence at the strategy table.
"Your many successes are invisible; your few mistakes are highly visible."	IT leaders don't feel like they get much recognition for their work. The public discussion always centers on their mistakes or problems.
"IT can make or break a company, but you are not a member of the corporate board."	IT leaders want "a seat at the table" and are searching to justify it.
"You run one of the most pervasive, critical functions, yet you must prove your value constantly."	IT leaders don't feel valued. Their budgets, plans and value-add are constantly questioned.
"You are intimately involved in every facet of the business, yet you are considered separate and apart from it."	IT leaders feel separate and apart. Many don't know how to be part of their organization.

What I hope you can see is that these paradoxes point more to the mindset and emotional disposition of IT leaders, and less to the inherently conflicting demands of the job.

But there's more

To combat these challenges many IT leaders have tried to market their way out of the problem. This response is so pervasive that the CIO Executive Council produced the "IT Internal Marketing Benchmark Study" to help members share best practices for marketing IT internally.

From this study we learn that the leading reason for undertaking internal marketing initiatives was "to better relationships with the rest of the organization," so that:

- "Internal customers seek out our assistance and don't work around us"
- "Technology projects are viewed as sound investments"

- "IT's importance is recognized and publicly acknowledged by executives"
- "IT is viewed as a source of innovation and thought leadership"

Leaving aside the obvious fact that you can't market your way to thought leadership, innovation and sound investments, the above listed desires are indicative of the pain being felt by IT leaders and their organizations.

Back to the man from Mars

So it seems that in fact the man from Mars isn't crazy at all. He sees quite clearly. And that brings me to the central question this book seeks to address: Why is this the case? What's going on?

- Why don't IT leaders feel appreciated and valued?
- Why are IT leaders often absent from critical decision making forums?
- Why don't IT leaders have a seat at the executive table? And most importantly,
- What can be done to change this situation?

The Journey | INFLUENCE: THE BIG IDEA

After 20+ years of working with some of the finest and most successful IT leaders on three continents, it is my firm conviction that the root cause of the problems faced by IT leaders in terms of access, respect, and value can all be traced to one key factor: INFLUENCE.

It is influence, or more accurately stated, the lack of influence, that is the root cause of so many of the management problems and frustrations expressed by IT leaders. It is a lack of influence that keeps IT leaders out of critical management forums. It is a lack of influence that prevents IT leaders from achieving their full professional potential. And it is a lack of influence that has IT leaders searching for answers to questions like:

- How do I change my company's attitude toward technology?
- How do I get more respect for the work the IT group does?
- How do I become more of an "insider"?
- How can I ensure my input and opinions are really heard?

Influence wielding – it's the IT leader's job

It's no surprise that influence is so important to IT leaders. To effectively do your job applying information technology to the needs of your company or organization requires that you influence your colleagues, peers, customers, stakeholders and bosses. That's what your organization needs you to do. That's what you are paid to do. And that's why it is so very frustrating for you to be without the influence you need to do a good job.

Think about it. You are constantly bombarded with ideas, suggestions, requests, requirements and needs of all sorts. You have to effectively influence your colleagues to make the right choices. Sometimes it is to invest in a specific infrastructure technology that only you understand. Other times it is to avoid a particular initiative because the associated implementation costs and time delays would exceed the anticipated business benefit. Regardless of the specifics of the situation, it's not hard to see the importance of influence for IT leaders.

This sense of the importance of influence to the job is echoed by many CIOs:

"Influence defines my job."
– Barbara Kunkel, CIO Troutman Sanders

"Without influence skills, CIOs are relegated to being order takers."
– Susan Cramm, Former CIO Taco Bell

"The influence I am privileged to enjoy with our senior management has helped our group accomplish a great deal."
– Akhil Tripathi, CIO Harleyville Mutual Insurance

Time and again I've found that it is influence that really makes the difference in the success of an IT leader and his group. IT leaders with influence are appreciated by their peers. Their opinions and ideas are respected and sought after, even beyond the area of IT.

Influential IT leaders are invited to join the senior decision making forums of their organizations. They are called upon to represent their organizations beyond the technology area per se. For example:

– Gerry McCartney, CIO of Purdue University is a member of the president's strategic cabinet and one of three university executives who presents to the board on academic research.

– Dave Barnes, CIO of UPS is a visionary spokesman for UPS. He frequently leads industry seminars on supply chain integration, innovation and environmentalism; not the typical stuff of your average CIO.

– Ken Lawonn, CIO of Alegent Health, a nine-hospital, 9,000 employee health-care system isn't just the CIO. He is also Senior VP in charge of the hospitals construction projects and retail business.

It goes beyond title and scope

IT leaders with influence not only enjoy a more fulfilling and engaged career experience, they make a lot of money! How much you ask? Well, I can't share all of the personal details I may know, but I can point out a few examples that should get you thinking about what's possible.

Within the last 24 months the following IT executives pay packages were reported in their company's public filings:

- Anna Ewing, NASDAQ/OMG Group - $2.8 million

- Steve Squeri, American Express - $6.8 million

- Robert B. Carter, Federal Express - $1.9 million

These executives may be at the high end of the scale, but they are an excellent example of what is possible. And from personal experience I can tell you that there are many IT leaders working in many different enterprises who enjoy very substantial compensation packages as a result of the value they create and the influence they command.

Net, net: There is great opportunity out there for IT leaders who know how to achieve and apply influence.

Why is influence missing for so many IT leaders?

The question you are likely asking yourself right now is why, if influence is so important, if it's the magic elixir to success as an IT leader, why isn't every IT leader out there working on this right now? Why is it so hard for IT leaders to build this competency?

Three substantial impediments have held back IT leaders from building the influence that is so important to them: They are:

1. **Awareness**
2. **Professional development gap**
3. **Aversion to the basic genre**

1. **Awareness.** Many IT leaders simply aren't aware they are playing a game of influence. They view influence as a skill, an important skill, but not as the central competency required for your success as an IT leader. (I hope I have succeeded in changing that a bit by now. Because shifting your awareness

regarding the importance of influence is the critical first step to addressing a lack of influence.)

2. **Professional development gap.** The second reason why IT leaders aren't well skilled in this area is because there isn't much relevant training or professional development to be found. Note—I said relevant. If you look at the training offerings in the area of influence building they tend to focus mostly on the sales roles or on personal development. There aren't any professional development programs on influence building specifically geared to the unique needs of IT leaders.

3. **Aversion to basic genre.** Third, and I think this is the most significant reason why IT leaders are not fully engaged in influence training, is that most IT leaders have an almost allergic reaction to the topic of influence building given the way it is often presented. And frankly, who can blame them? Most of the material feels very manipulative in nature. Take a look at the titles of some of the best selling books in this category:

   - *How to Win Friends and Influence People*
     Dale Carnegie
   - *Get Anyone to Do Anything*
     David J. Lieberman
   - *The Science of Influence: How to get Anyone to say YES in 8 Minutes or Less*
     Kevin Hogan
   - *Maximum Influence: The 12 Universal Laws of Power Persuasion*
     Kurt Mortensen

Just a quick glance makes professionally-minded IT leaders break out in a rash. That's because most of these books (and seminars) come across as being so self-serving; seemingly about getting your way with other people. And that sort of approach doesn't sit well with scientifically-minded IT leaders, who are used to letting their work speak for itself.

IT professionals are generally wary of fast-talking techniques and methods to prove value. That feels a lot like the vendors they have to fend off on a regular basis. They prefer to prove value by delivering value, not by giving a slick presentation (frankly that's a good thing).

IT people believe that it is systems and deliverables that are supposed to demonstrate value, not "persuasion" per se. It's therefore no surprise that they are not drawn to this type of material.

But it doesn't have to be that way. In fact, it shouldn't be that way at all.

How IT leaders *should* think about influence

There is another genre of influence besides the "what's in it for me" variety. It's the kind of influence that's referred to when we speak to our kids and we tell them we want them to be "an influence for good." It's an influence that is rooted in a desire to shape or give direction toward a positive outcome—to have a positive effect on what people do or experience.

This genre of influence is not about "getting your way" but rather about having the appropriate sway to ensure that the right things happen in the IT realm for which you are responsible.

Sometimes that means using your influence to ensure that software standards are maintained to prevent run-away support costs. Other times you may need to use your influence to stop a project that you know won't ever succeed, despite the enthusiasm shown by the user community. Whatever it may be, it's about putting your influence to work in order to do the right thing in the IT arena. That is, after all, your job.

From creating a technology strategy and prioritizing between competing organizational requirements, to supporting a software vendor choice, nearly everything you do requires the ability to effectively influence your colleagues, peers, customers, stakeholders or boss.

It's an appropriate and ethical influence. It's exactly the kind of influence you need to do your job well. And most importantly, it's the kind of influence you should feel very comfortable pursuing.

But before we get started on the journey through *The Secrets* that will give you this influence, I'll address one more question...

The Journey | WHY I WROTE THIS BOOK

Like many of you reading this book, I have a classical background in computer science and I spent many years implementing large-scale business management systems. I got my start writing code, performing analyses and then moved on to project management and oversight positions. I worked for a couple of different companies eventually working my way up to partner at PricewaterhouseCoopers, and then leading a global consulting practice area for IBM; before establishing my own boutique firm in 2003.

I first became aware of the importance of influence for IT leaders early on in my professional career. As part of a team charged with implementing large and complex systems, I was often assigned to work with the senior executive team. My role was to tease out the vision of the senior management and to ensure the project was well aligned with the company's goals and strategy.

Early on my peers and bosses pointed out that I seemed to have a knack for capturing and keeping the attention of the executive suite. Somehow, I managed to secure and keep the support of the senior executives for very complex IT projects. What's more, as a result of my interaction with the senior executives in one area of technology, they often spoke with me about other technology-related questions and issues. They were interested in learning about how technology could impact their business, and I seemed to have their ear.

Putting influence to work

It was at that point that my career really took off. Because I used the influence and access that I had with the senior executives of the company to support the needs of the CIO and the technology group who were my direct clients.

Pretty soon CIOs and other senior IT leaders were hiring me and my firm because they saw the access and influence I was able to acquire and they wanted to be able to both leverage it more broadly and learn how to get it themselves. And so my focus slowly shifted from gaining access and influence for myself and for my specific project, to helping CIOs and their teams build this type of access and influence for themselves to achieve their fuller agendas.

I noticed how critical this issue of influence was. And so I started to pay much closer attention to how people achieved influence. Not only did I pay much closer attention to my own tactics and strategies but I started to carefully observe and research the tactics and strategies of the many IT leaders with whom I came into contact.

At first I had little more than intuition to go on. But with time I noticed certain patterns of behavior emerging in critical IT management contexts, such as when an IT leader is seeking to:

- Promote an idea or project

- Deliver complex information or bad news

- Achieve agreement with an IT strategy

- Gain approval for a budget increase

- Build a strong relationship with a business colleague

In these, and similar situations, I started to notice that certain patterns of behavior turned out to be pretty reliable indicators of whether or not a particular IT leader would succeed in their endeavors and build influence or not.

The patterns ranged from the silly and symbolic (like not crouching under the conference room table and fiddling with the wires when the projector isn't working) to the esoteric and intellectual (like achieving external recognition to improve internal respect). Slowly a picture began to emerge. As I began to see more clearly, I placed more emphasis on noticing, documenting and testing out these patterns.

It started with projects

At first I put these ideas to work in a straight-forward project context by helping my clients to: (1) sell their ideas and projects more effectively and, (2) ensure their senior management stayed aligned and "in the boat" with them throughout the course of the project. This worked well and I enjoyed watching my clients succeed not only with their projects, but with their careers.

A CRM rollout became less about a new customer management system and more about an opportunity to make an IT leader and his team shine. A chance to highlight the tremendous contribution the IT team was making to the success of the company. And a new analytics system became the vehicle for galvanizing the IT group into a high-performing insight delivery team, valued and appreciated by their marketing peers.

I was able to shift my focus from projects and deliverables to people and their achievements. Best of all, not only were the IT leaders doing better, but their companies were getting much better value from their technology investments. It was a real win-win.

From projects to strategy and leadership

It was rewarding and fun, but doing this work on a project-by-project basis was also tiring. Thankfully, it didn't take long for me to realize that there was a better way.

Rather than applying these ideas and concepts on a one-off basis, the more effective way to establish and grow the influence of the IT team was to weave the disciplines of influence into the very fabric of the IT group. In other words, build it into the core IT strategy and management disciplines. And that's exactly what I did.

Working with talented IT leaders from around the world (many of whom you will meet in the upcoming pages) I was able to hone and refine these ideas and techniques into a new arsenal of influence-building tools, techniques and approaches to the classical and persistent challenges facing IT leaders.

As my clients put these ideas and techniques to work within their groups, they began to see big changes in the outcomes they experienced. I had the opportunity to watch my clients, good, hard-working people, succeed in their careers. I saw my clients successfully win approval from their bosses, get promoted, secure raises, and take a seat at the executive table. Most importantly, I observed many of my clients experience an improvement in their personal work experience and how they felt about their role.

Reality bites

This experience was personally and professionally rewarding. But over the last few years several developments in the IT industry began to gnaw at me. I was pained, really pained by the way in which the world of the IT professional and IT leader was being painted:

- The steady chorus of voices proclaiming the diminished importance of IT in the corporate arena.

- Exaggerated expectations of outsourcing and the attendant notion that IT leadership is becoming less relevant.

- The proliferation of articles and surveys (like those I shared with you earlier in this book) pointing to the wide-scale feelings of diminished value and lack of respect felt by IT leaders.

I was (and still am) bothered by the persistently negative views of the IT community. But most of all, I was pained by the lack of satisfaction and self-actualization that so many IT leaders seemed to be experiencing.

I understood where it was coming from, but I also knew that conventional wisdom was dead wrong on this one; that it didn't have to be this way for so many people.

The particularly tough part for me was that while I heard lots of people talking about the problems, I didn't really hear any real-world, proven and workable solutions. A lot of pie-in-sky ideas, yes. But down-to-earth practical solutions were in short supply.

But I knew the reasons for the problems being felt by IT leaders and I knew the solutions that would help them.

So out of respect and thanks to the many IT leaders who have helped me along the way and as a small payback for all that I have gained from the IT community, I decided it was time to lend a hand and help fix things. I decided to write this book. To put down on paper all that I had learned and see work so effectively for so many IT leaders around the world.

Once I got started

I realized that I had a important responsibility and opportunity. Because as helpful and insightful as my experiences over the last 20 + years may be, they were still a rather small statistical sample. For the information in this book to enjoy mainstream acceptance I knew it needed to be supported by up-to-date research and surveys. So that's exactly what I did.

For nearly two years, I worked with my research team updating our knowledgebase. We integrated materials from new publications and studies on the nature of influence. We reached out to IT leaders with whom we had no relationship to solicit their input, feedback and peer review. We conducted numerous surveys. We made sure we had the data to support our experiences.

And then finally

After all the research was done we had one final task before us: To assemble all the material, lessons, insights, teachings and stories into a truly meaningful structure, so that IT leaders like you could put it straight to work. After all, that's why I wrote this book: To help you right now, right away. Not to add a new volume of theoretical approaches to IT management for the academic community to review and discuss, but rather to put a real-world road map in your hands right now.

I wrote this book in order to give you the tools to dramatically change your professional experience. Not to show you a trick or two, but rather to expose you to methods that can fundamentally alter the way in which you operate in your enterprise and the incredible results it can bring.

It's my hope that if enough IT leaders put the information revealed in this book to work, not only will we see a new wave of positively-oriented articles appearing in the industry press, but there will also be a lot more satisfied and well-compensated IT leaders across the globe. And all of you, the professional managers who bring trillions of dollars of value to the world economy through the effective deployment, operation and management of technology, will start to enjoy the influence and respect you truly deserve.

The Journey | **THE 11 SECRETS INFLUENCE-BUILDING ROAD MAP**

How *The Secrets* are organized

While researching and writing this book, I was concerned about how best to convey this information so that it wouldn't just come across as a list. I wanted the reader to be able to see the connections and dependencies between the different secrets. To get a sense of how all the individual pieces fit together and form a unified idea.

I wrestled with different approaches (such as by context or by subject area). In the end I chose to organize *The Secrets* in the form of a journey with a road map. That journey is made up of three parts. Each part contains a number of steps (*The Secrets*) that logically build one upon another. In this way, you get not only *The Secrets* themselves, but a clear pathway for putting them to work.

Part I, Influence Begins with Credibility teaches you the key activities and behaviors you need to set in place a foundation of credibility—the basis for influence. On the surface, the idea of credibility as a foundation to influence seems rather obvious. What *The Secrets* reveal however is that the path to credibility is often misunderstood by the very best IT leaders. Many devoted IT leaders work hard at delivering great systems, yet still find themselves without real credibility and influence. Part I explains (a) the common misunderstandings that give rise to this situation, (b) what you can do to avoid it, and (c) how to effectively build credibility.

Once you have implemented the key activities and behaviors contained in Part I (or if you are there already) you move on to *Part II, The Essentials of Influential Communications.* Part II clarifies the biggest area of challenge faced by most IT leaders. More importantly, it reveals a number of very unconventional secrets that you can use to quickly improve your standing and influence with your bosses and peers.

Part III, Game Time, focuses on the critical situations and contexts where you, as the IT leader, have the opportunity to shine. Part III builds on what is taught in Parts I and II and teaches specific tactics to use in order to be successful in these very important professional situations.

The 11 Secrets Influence-Building Road Map

The road map on the following pages provides a visual guide to *The Secrets.* Beyond the obvious road signs, the road map contains a number of hints and subtleties about the secrets. As you become familiar with the each of the secrets, you will find the road map a more informative and useful reference tool.

Before you begin your journey

If you want to give yourself the very best chance of successfully implementing the concepts in this book, don't jump right into the secrets just yet. Before you set out on your journey, before you are exposed to anything new, take stock of where you are right now. Take a few minutes and do a quick assessment of where your influence currently stands.

To help you with that assessment, I invite you to use one of our on-line assessment tools. You can find it here:

<u>https://www.marcjschiller.com/influence-assessment/</u>

The assessment score and the accompanying qualitative analysis will provide you with: (1) an initial benchmark against which you can measure your results over time, and (2) pointers and foreknowledge of the areas that will be most relevant and beneficial to you. This will support your journey through *The Secrets.*

OK, let's go.

The **11 Secrets** Road Map

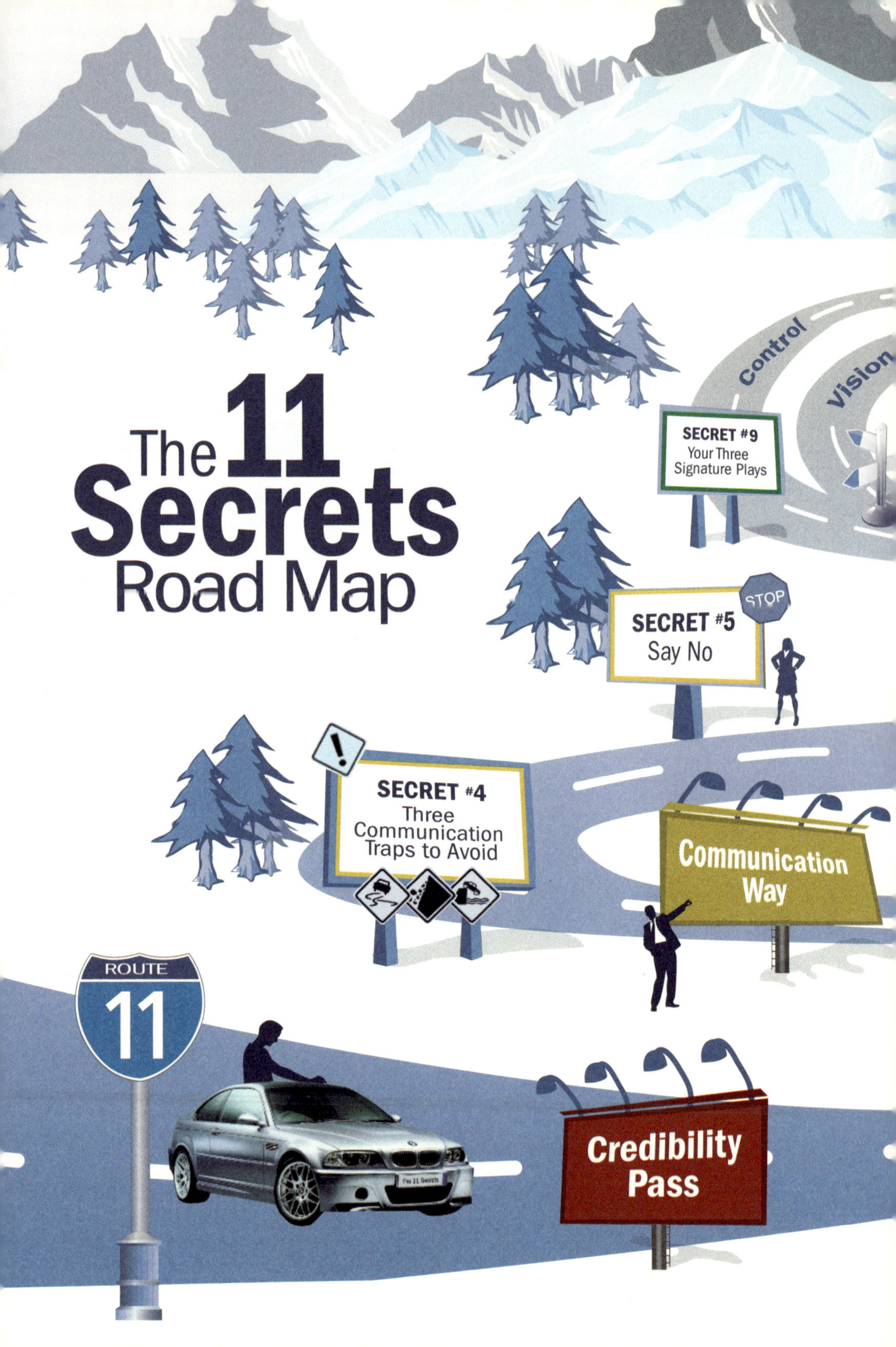
The 11 Secrets
Road Map
Control
Vision
SECRET #9
Your Three
Signature Plays
SECRET #5
Say No
STOP
SECRET #4
Three
Communication
Traps to Avoid
Communication
Way
ROUTE
11
Credibility
Pass

Welcome to
INFLUENCE
(city limits)

SECRET #10
Get Your Team
to Really Play

SECRET #11
Take your Game
on the Road

egy

SECRET #8
You Gotta Know
the Game

ROUGH TERRAIN
AHEAD

Game Time
Highway

SECRET #7
Practice
"Ne-ma-wa-shi"

SECRET #6
Be Skeptical

THE GATEWAY TO TRUST
Process
Strategies
Financial
Proximal

SECRET #3
Business
Intimacy

SECRET #1
Infrastructure
Really Matters

TUNE UP

SECRET #2
Expect Projects
to Fail

DETOUR

PART I

INFLUENCE BEGINS WITH CREDIBILITY

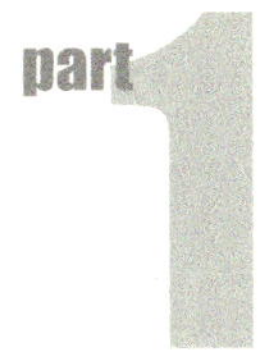

Secret #1: Infrastructure Really Matters

Secret #2: Expect Projects to Fail

Secret #3: Business Intimacy – The Gateway to Trust

Rock-solid credibility is the bedrock upon which influence stands. In order to influence your colleagues, peers, customers, stakeholders, and boss, you must possess a strong degree of credibility with them. Without credibility, even the simplest of things can be nearly impossible to get done.

Part I opens a door into the unique perspective and approach taken by highly influential IT leaders on how to build credibility.

SECRET #1

INFRASTRUCTURE REALLY MATTERS

"IT is a lot like plumbing. People don't want to hear how it works or why it works; they just want to know that it does work."

Christopher Barron
CIO, CP Energy

Influential IT leaders know that the absolute, foundational, number-one, most important thing they can do to establish and maintain their credibility—and thereby lay a foundation for influence—is get their core infrastructure and operations humming.

The common trap is to think that influential IT leaders are busy doing big, important projects—that the best IT leaders aren't really worried about infrastructure and pipes—as if that's for the "nerds." Nothing could be farther from the truth.

I find that the most influential IT leaders recognize how critical infrastructure is to their mission and by extension to their credibility. They invest considerable time and resources to ensure that core IT services are delivered flawlessly. They carefully and purposefully overprovision bandwidth, server power, storage space, communications and support resources. In budget meetings, they fight tooth and nail for leading-edge infrastructure.

Bandwidth beats beauty

Take the story of Joanne Kossuth. She is the Vice President for Operations and CIO of Franklin W. Olin College of Engineering in Needham, Mass. She reports directly to the President of the College, is a member of the executive committee and in addition to her IT responsibilities she is charged with overseeing: campus services, conference services, dining services, facilities, human resources, planning and project management, public safety, and purchasing.

When the college was first being built, Joanne realized she had a unique opportunity to put in place a growth-oriented and flexible infrastructure. She knew that once the buildings and physical plant were largely in place, the costs and opportunities for opening walls and running new lines would be limited. So she decided to push the infrastructure investment to the limit.

Listening to her tell the story you get a sense of how clear her vision was about the importance of infrastructure.

> "As an engineering and technical college I knew our professors and students would always be pushing the limits of technology. And even if I couldn't exactly predict where and how the technology would be used, I knew it would be needed soon enough. So I pushed forward with major investments in fiber optics, physical plant wiring, communications and networking systems. We committed to VOIP long before it was a mainstream technology and assumed a nearly limitless appetite for internet bandwidth.

> Sure enough, it wasn't long before our budgets were being strained. But I knew that I had to have the fight now because otherwise the college (and IT) would pay the price many times over the coming years.

> So I went to meet with the president of the college. He was very adamant about sticking to the budget. But I wouldn't relent. I just kept emphasizing for him how critical the IT infrastructure was for the very mission of the college. That it went way beyond providing the basics necessary to run computer systems.

> Finally he said: Joanne, we simply don't have the money. For me to give you the money for these computer systems means I can't put stone facing on the administration buildings. It will be very hard to convince our benefactors that the money for the beautiful buildings instead went into the IT infrastructure. I told him it was worth every penny and that the benefactors would thank him many times over the next few years. I can't say for sure if they ever did. But he has certainly thanked me for pushing him on this."

What's the big deal

On the surface the casual observer might wonder what's the big deal? Invest in infrastructure and run the systems well. Big deal. That's what every IT leader has to do. It's just part of the day-to-day operations. What's the big secret here?

The secret lies in recognizing three things: First, what it means to have well-running IT infrastructure. Second, where infrastructure matters most for your organization. And third, applying it correctly.

Unfortunately, we have grown accustomed to help desk delays, networking issues and other manifestations of poor IT infrastructure performance. As a result, the bar for well-run infrastructure has been lowered considerably in the minds of too many IT professionals. We have become too forgiving of IT because we know how technically complex all this stuff really is. But our user community doesn't know and doesn't care.

To understand what top-notch infrastructure really means you have to get into the mindset of your user community, in particular the senior executives at your company or organization.

Simply stated, they want everything to work perfectly all of the time. They want super fast internet connectivity wherever they may be. They want access to perfectly replicated email on their computers at home, in the office, on the road and their mobile devices (yes, multiple devices). And more than what they do want, is what they don't want.

They don't want to hear from their admin staff that the systems are slow and there will be a delay in sending them a file on the road. They don't want to hear from other senior executives that due to system downtime they had to pay $200,000 in overtime costs to process orders. They don't want to hear that server overloads caused the website to go down for two hours the previous week (at just the time the new board member went to look at the company website.) And they don't want to have to call tech support—for anything.

Think about it. Do you think they ever want to talk to a tech support person? Does anyone? In the mind of your senior executives, top-notch IT systems should never break. I know that sounds crazy, but that is what your colleagues really want. ZERO problems of any sort. And if they do have a problem they want it fixed by an expert immediately. No explaining, no troubleshooting, no escalating, no callbacks, and no expectation management. Just their problem fixed right away, right now.

All of those pesky and so-called "unimportant" tech support calls for printers not working or SPAM problems with email are glaring examples of less-than-perfect operating infrastructure.

Too high of a standard? Too much to expect from technology? Absolutely correct. And, absolutely irrelevant. Because that's how your user community thinks.

Highly influential IT leaders recognize that this expectation is unrealistic, but they never for a moment forget that this is the expectation. And so they apply as much high-end infrastructure as possible to shore up the systems and head off as many of these common problems as possible.

Why infrastructure and operations really matter

There are two big reasons why tending to matters of infrastructure and operations are so critical to establishing credibility and influence as an IT leader. First, is the fact that in the mind of your user community, you are the systems. Second, the very large dollars spent in this area.

You are the systems. For your user community your personal credibility is measured in direct proportion to the performance of the systems. If the systems and support are running well, then you are wonderful. If the systems are down and problematic, then you are a bum and an incompetent. This may be totally unfair, but it is absolutely the case.

This is especially true in the executive suite where they are totally clueless about all of the technical difficulties involved in running an IT shop, and where they are not exposed to the many "cool" systems you may have implemented to help the business. For the executive suite, it's their personal experience of the most basic aspects of IT that often determines how you are perceived as an IT leader.

Christopher Barron, CIO at CP Energy sums it very crisply:

> "For most people, IT is what they can see, touch, feel. We might be investing tens of millions of dollars in big ERP systems, but the most interaction the average executive will have with IT is with regard to his Blackberry or laptop. So all those things have to be really stable, and as cutting-edge as we can afford.
>
> I never underestimate the value of desktop technology, smart phone technology, or anything else a person interacts with on a daily basis."

The money. In addition to the day-to-day interaction executives have with basic infrastructure technologies and operations, the executive suite sees how much money is being spent on IT infrastructure. And if your IT department is like most, that infrastructure number is probably pretty big—often 80% or more of the IT budget. Accordingly, the executive suite thinks that if you can't effectively manage the big budget items (i.e., the infrastructure and operations that are under your control and provide crisp service) then how can you be taken seriously as a business leader?

Another mistake made by many IT leaders is that they believe the IT infrastructure budget line is viewed by the senior executives as basic company operations, like plant and building infrastructure. That the only real IT spending is the investment in new technologies and applications and that their financial and management focus need only be on this area.

Executives do expect technology to be as reliable and trouble-free as other types of infrastructure, but this in no way takes away from the expectation that the IT leader have very firm control over that budget. Any attempt to marginalize infrastructure, and its importance on how you are viewed as an IT leader is a mistake.

Not all infrastructures matter in the same way

Influential IT leaders recognize that the smooth running of core infrastructure/operations, and in particular those elements that touch senior executives, directly impacts their personal credibility and the overall credibility of the IT group. But it doesn't stop there. Influential IT leaders recognize that with limited budgets they need to carefully consider in which areas of infrastructure to invest most substantially.

For some organizations, it's all about the network and communications bandwidth. For others it's about security and disaster recovery. For one company, the key infrastructure investments are the huge server farms that host its web-based application service. For another company, it's dedicated tech-support services for highly compensated financial traders that matter most. Sure, there are basic infrastructure needs that are common to most organizations. But no company can go all out investing at the high end for every type of infrastructure.

So what's an IT leader supposed to do given this situation? What infrastructure investments provide good ROI in terms of building credibility and influence without breaking the bank? Clearly it varies based on the nature of your organization and where your senior executives are most likely to bump into infrastructure issues. And while there aren't a set of hard and fast rules, the following guidelines should provide you with a good starting point.

1. **Over provision key services and technologies that directly impact user productivity.** Most common examples include: internet bandwidth, mailbox storage, and disk storage. But remember to be sensitive to your industry's unique needs. For example in the financial community traders and other screen-based personnel are given multiple, large, high-quality display monitors.

2. **Invest in user experience infrastructure.** Nearly every system has a user-facing component; typically it's called the user interface or the front end of the system. It's typically the last piece of the application that gets put into place once the "back end," guts of the system are working properly. And while the heavy lifting may be happening in the back end, it's the front end that the user community experiences. And that experience should be as friction-free and enjoyable as possible. Invest in whatever additional infrastructure may be necessary to deliver a highly reliable and pleasant user experience. Conventional wisdom says make sure the back end is right because the front end is easy to tweak. That may be the case, but while you're busy tweaking the front end and feeling like a success because the back end is rock solid, your colleagues are gossiping about the "crappy system" and all the front-end issues they have encountered.

3. **Provide high-touch user support as far down the organization as economically possible.** It may be common sense to make sure the CEO doesn't have email problems, but it can't stop there. All of the senior leaders in your company should be receiving VIP support for their personal computers. And it's probably a good idea to include their assistants as well. If possible, continue to extend this level of support down the organizational hierarchy. Maybe the ratio of support personnel to users increases, but at least there is a live desk-side person available within a reasonable amount of time, not just a voice on the end of the phone.

   Here is a great example:

How Mike Saft saves the day (several times a week)

When I speak of infrastructure, I want to make very clear that I'm speaking not only about the core technologies themselves, i.e., the software and hardware that make up the systems, but also of the support services. In fact, in many cases it's the support services that matter more than the technologies themselves. Investing in the very best systems but skimping on the support personnel that run them is a recipe for disaster. On the other hand, thoughtful investment in high-end technologies along with the right support personnel can work wonders. The story of Mike Saft of Bayer Business Technology Services (BBTS) tells it best.

First, a little background. BBTS is the internal technology services provider for Bayer companies. Working alongside the IT leaders within the business units, BBTS provides much of the day-to-day operational services for Bayer companies. From network connectivity to SAP support, BBTS is the primary address to which Bayer employees turn for help.

Mike Saft is a warm and friendly technology maven with the rather unique job title of VIP Customer Support Specialist. His primary assignments: (1) To support the senior commercial leaders of Bayer Healthcare Pharmaceuticals, and (2) To ensure the smooth running of all projection systems and other AV equipment in the executive building in Wayne, New Jersey.

Mike is situated on-site with the executive team ready to respond to any technology issues they may have. What's more, he is on site to make sure that presentations, video conferences, training, town hall meetings, and any other gathering that uses the built-in audio visual equipment, comes off without a problem.

It's not that BBTS doesn't have comprehensive help desk facilities that could support the managers and executives at the Wayne location. Nor is it the case that the projection and A/V systems lack detailed documentation for self-service. Rather, BBTS has made a strategic decision to over provision support resources in these two critical areas. And if you have ever visited Bayer's Wayne, New Jersey facility and met Mike Saft, it's real easy to see what a smart decision that is.

Mike is the archetype support specialist. He knows the systems he supports inside and out and he really cares about making things work well for his colleagues. He is the consummate professional and he takes great care in not only making things work, but in how he interacts with everyone. Whether in a conference room with a meeting for three people or in the auditoriums holding hundreds of people, Mike is always at the ready to make sure things work smoothly.

Obviously BBTS can't invest like this in every area, but given the importance of the US pharmaceutical business, it's not hard to appreciate the wisdom of having Mike there for the managers and executives who run that business.

The result

When I look at the organizations of highly influential IT leaders that have put this principle to work, I usually find:

1. A generally more friction-free, information-processing environment. People tend to be more comfortable with their day-to-day use of systems and experience less tension about systems and their operations.

2. Users report greater productivity. Less time is spent dealing with common system issues. An ability to get to work and keep working without technology-based interruptions

3. Users feel that IT knows what it is doing. They talk about a sense of calm and control and the ability to rely on IT to keep things running. Frequently they will cite examples such as quick laptop swap outs with no data loss or proactive system upgrades to make their point.

So what happens when you get it right? What is the pay off for IT leaders?

Larry Bonfante, CIO of the U.S. Tennis Association, spent a great deal of time and energy getting infrastructure technologies and services humming. As a result of this work he reports:

> "Over the last couple of years we've been able to broaden our scope of influence beyond IT. We've taken on a number of other functional responsibilities, because we are seen as people who know how to deliver and support any kind of customer service-related function."

One last challenge to conventional wisdom

It's not uncommon for the press or the so-called "experts" to rail about the non-strategic nature of infrastructure. Often we hear it said that to claim your place in the executive suite you need to leave that techie stuff behind and focus on more strategic items. Well, news flash: infrastructure is only non-strategic when it's working flawlessly. When it's not working flawlessly, all of a sudden it becomes a critical item. And if the problems persist, it's a real credibility killer for IT leaders. So think 100 times before shifting investment and attention away from infrastructure because the "experts" are telling you it's not so sexy or important.

EXPECT PROJECTS TO FAIL

"When people began to realize that they could count on me to deliver on my commitments—that helped me to develop influence with the senior team at AWC."

Dale Franz, CIO
Auto Warehousing Co.

Generally speaking, IT leaders separate their work into two areas: (1) infrastructure and operations (which we just covered), and (2) projects.

The term "projects" generally refers to new systems initiatives taking place—some of which will eventually become part of core operational systems. But projects aren't only systems work per se. In fact, many IT projects only have paper deliverables such as in the case of a feasibility study, a requirements analysis, a process definition, a business case, a review of system operations, whatever it might be.

Projects is a catch-all label refering to any and all work to produce something that is not presently part of day-to-day operations. Projects have a specific and tangible end-goal or deliverable in mind due within a specific timeframe.

Although infrastructure and operations tend to consume the lion's share of the IT budget, it's the projects, especially those high-profile, sexy sounding projects, where a great deal of executive attention is focused. And since the projects are often expensive and important to the user community, they typically are subject to a great deal of interest and scrutiny.

So it's in the project arena where most IT leaders naturally believe that their credibility is most on the line. They reason, and rightly so, that they can't possibly have any credibility with the senior executives without a solid track record of successful project delivery.

So far, pretty reasonable thinking. But the problem is that this concern for a solid track record of successful project delivery doesn't stop there. For many IT leaders it translates into a desire to see to it that every IT project is doing well at every moment in time. What's more—and this is the really dangerous part—many IT leaders believe that in the tradition of "the buck stops here" they need to take personal responsibility for every IT project.

What's wrong with this approach?

This mindset and approach to project work yields a number of unfortunate outcomes. First, it leads to over involvement by the IT leader. In an effort to stem any project issue, IT leaders often get too personally involved in how a project is running.

Second, this mindset causes IT leaders to take over the communication of project status to key stakeholders. In an effort to control the "spin" related to project status, IT leaders take on communications roles that are best left to others. This in turn leads to the third big problem with this approach: It sets up the IT leader's credibility to move in tandem with the day-to-day shifts in project status.

Being so clearly identified with the project, the IT leader unwittingly ties his personal credibility not to the overall track record of the IT group over time, but to the day-to-day status of the particular project about which he is communicating at any given moment.

But the most important reason why this approach to project work is faulty, is because IT projects fail. That's right; try as we might, IT projects fail. It's just a cold hard fact of systems work. Some projects simply do not succeed. So, if you are counting on a perfect track record in project delivery to build your credibility, you are probably in for a serious disappointment. It's simply not a realistic goal. And that's the basis of *Secret #2*.

Highly influential IT leaders recognize that not every project can be a success. More bluntly stated, they expect projects to fail. And it is that recognition, and what they do about it, that together make up the essence of *Secret #2*.

Why influential IT leaders expect projects to fail

The answer is pretty simple: because they have experience. And they know that's just the way it goes, especially in technology; even more so if you occasionally push the envelope a bit.

Some projects fail for "good" reasons like:

- The technology isn't ready for prime time

- The user community is not committed enough

- Budget estimations were made under a different business climate

- Investment resources have changed

In other cases, IT projects fail for what are conventionally considered "bad" reasons, such as:

- The promised functionality wasn't delivered

- Poor overall performance of the system

- Poor design or implementation

- Over budget, over time

The truth is that the reason for the failure almost doesn't matter. If you are going to have credibility and influence, you are going to have to find a way to build it given the reality that IT projects fail. The question is how to do it.

Now before I answer that question, let me clarify. Clearly you can't attain substantial influence within your organization when IT projects are failing on a regular basis. And I do not mean to suggest that influential IT leaders don't work their hardest to make every project successful; of course they do.

What I do mean however, is that in order to navigate the rocky waters of IT project delivery, influential IT leaders adopt an approach that is firmly rooted in the reality that projects are going to fail. And given that reality, they configure their behavior and interactions with their colleagues accordingly.

Let's take a closer look at how this works...

Dealing with reality

In *Secret #1*, I pointed out the very common attitude held by your stakeholder community that you are the systems. And as it pertains to running a tight operation and infrastructure, there is no way to avoid this association. In fact, you need to embrace it.

However, when it comes to project work, what I am suggesting is different. With project work, because of its very nature, it is a potential disaster for your credibility to be directly tied to the outcome of every single project. It's not that you are running away from management responsibility. It's just that you are going to avoid tying your personal credibility to the ups and downs of the various IT projects—for which you are ultimately responsible, but not directly managing. Instead you are going to connect your credibility (and by extension influence) to your personal commitments regarding overall project oversight and governance; which is where you essentially operate.

If it feels a bit like a difficult dance, then you are getting it, because it is.

Sure it would be easier to just stand up and say that as the IT leader you are responsible for making every project a success and standing by it. The problem is that rarely works, and is in direct conflict with reality.

Given that projects are going to fail, what do highly influential IT leaders do in order to build credibility? In a nutshell, they build their *personal credibility* on their *personal commitments*—**not** on the day-to-day deliverables of the IT project portfolio. They decouple their personal reputation and credibility from the ups and downs of each and every IT project. They keep a healthy and appropriate personal distance between themselves and the projects. In other words, they do not offer up their reputation and credibility based on the twists and turns of every IT project being performed in their organization. Instead, they make a clear distinction between their personal commitments and the project specifics.

This is not to say that they don't care about the projects. They do, very much. It's just that they take a very professional and objective approach to the projects. They leave enough space between themselves and the projects so that the project can have a life of its own. And that way as the IT leader they have enough space to properly review, criticize, and sometimes even cancel the project without it being a personal credibility killer.

How to make the shift

Highly influential IT leaders use a number of tactics and methods to effectively create the appropriate space between their personal credibility and the day-to-day challenges of IT projects. In particular, they:

1. **Manage expectations.** From the very start, i.e., from day one on the job, highly influential IT leaders make the point that unpleasant and undesirable as it may be, IT projects fail. They school their colleagues in this reality and instill in them a realistic sense about the nature of technology projects. As projects progress they avoid making promises and telling everyone how great things will be once the new system is in place. They openly demonstrate concern and point out what could go wrong and they adopt the voice of calm and reason. They try to soften the gung-ho, "let's do it!" enthusiasm of less-experienced IT professionals and their counterparts in the business.

2. **Sweat the money.** Highly influential IT leaders always, always, always stay on top of the financial situation and ramifications of a project. They make sure to have a clear understanding of every little financial detail so the finance people never catch them off-guard. In fact, they seek out an active alliance with finance to ensure they are never surprised. Nothing says you are a serious businessperson like demonstrating you have a firm hand on the finances.

3. **Let others present the project.** No matter the forum, when it comes to presenting a project and its status, that job is best handled by the project manager or the department head under which the project falls. As the IT leader you should not be the person delivering the status report or project update to the executive management team, steering committee or user community. Highly influential IT leaders are careful to retain the position of thoughtful overseeing executive. They take a seat alongside their business peers which enables them to support their people making the presentation and at the same time maintain their position as an overseeing executive.

4. **Focus on risk management, governance and change management.** These three areas are nearly always the make-or-break items for every IT project. By concentrating on these critical areas, influential IT leaders shift their position from head project manager—responsible for perfect performance on all projects—to the highly concerned and involved leader focused on ensuring project success.

5. **Make and keep *personal* commitments.** Whether it's validating a business case, securing additional resources or conducting an audit, influential IT leaders make sure their colleagues know when they are making a personal commitment and when they do, they don't drop the ball. The project may be having a tough time delivering a particular outcome, but influential IT leaders always deliver on their personal commitments.

Sum up

Sure it's great to get some cool projects done on-time and on-budget. But that's pretty much what everyone expects of you anyway. The challenge of IT project work is navigating the gulf between that expectation and the reality that IT projects can and do fail.

Secret #2, Expect Projects to Fail, challenges you to bring this reality to the forefront of your credibility-building efforts.

BUSINESS INTIMACY – THE GATEWAY TO TRUST

"My staff resides at the line-of-business locations. At the headquarters of the DMV, I have a key manager and about 65 staff; they're in the cubicle right next door to the customer. Same thing with my motor carrier group; I have about 20 staff at their division. Same thing with highway transportation—just over 100 people there."

Ben Berry, CIO
Oregon Department of Transportation

Many IT leaders mistakenly assume that it is their position, knowledge and experience with IT that forms the basis of their credibility and influence. For the minority of managers that realize that these items count for very little with their colleagues, they expect their track record of meeting their commitments (see *Secret #2*) and running a smooth IT operation (see *Secret #1*) to more than qualify them for a seat at the table on important business issues. Unfortunately, experience and the story of Richard J., senior vice-president of information technology at a $2 billion dollar publishing firm, teaches us that it just doesn't work like that.

When everything looks right, but isn't – Richard's story

I first met Richard at an industry conference a few years ago. A common friend introduced us over drinks at an evening mixer. As he introduced us (and then stepped away) he told Richard that I would enjoy his story, but that I would be especially interested in his problem. With that, he left us to chat.

Richard and his team were under a great deal of pressure from the senior management of their company. Like almost all publishing companies, their print-based business model was under attack from the Internet. Their board had approved a $50 million multi-year IT investment to create a new platform for integrated multi-media publishing with specific emphasis on: (1) streamlining content development and distribution, and (2) enhancing on-line advertising opportunities.

I found the work that Richard was doing to be fascinating—particularly in the area of componentizing and re-purposing content. I couldn't help myself. I was full of questions about his projects and his vision for the new business model and the role of IT. It was a wonderful conversation; at least it was for me.

As the conversation wore on, I noticed Richard slowly losing enthusiasm; every now and then expressing frustration about the likelihood of it ever really working. In particular he had doubts about the business people adapting to the new business model and to the heavily system-driven approach. Something was not quite right and I remembered our mutual friend's comment about his "problem." What initially sounded to me like a very well thought-out strategy followed by early deployment success (albeit self-reported) wasn't the full story. Richard was clearly uncomfortable with the program. Something was wrong.

By this point we had spoken for nearly an hour and the free flowing drinks helped to inspire even greater honesty in our conversation. (Don't laugh. You've been to these industry events with the vendor-sponsored cocktail hours and dinners. This stuff happens all the time.)

I'm a big fan of the straightforward approach so I just came right out with it and asked, "Richard, what's with the negative attitude? You're doing such cool stuff, so tightly aligned to the strategic business needs of your company, why all the worry and concern about the business community? What's the problem?"

His answer went something like this:

"I can't quite put my finger on what's wrong, but there are a few troubling signs. For example: it takes the business community too long to get back to us on small issues.

We develop using tight modules and very purposefully manage scope. We don't require long, drawn-out design meetings. Yet when we send simple questions by email, on things like UI layouts, it can take days to get an answer.

One of the most irritating things is the constant questioning and look of surprise I get from the executive oversight team at the costs of the program. It's not like they haven't been briefed on this 100 times already. Yet it seems like they keep asking nearly the same questions every time.

Another example is what we have come to call the "out of the blue syndrome." After spending a substantial amount of time in design and prototyping and just as we are ready to go into alpha testing, "out of the blue" the business users will bring up some super critical issue about the business direction, or they will revise the basic process model.

I'm not talking about a tweak or refinement. I mean a substantial difference that requires rethinking basic assumptions. I often find myself wondering, 'where have you been all this time'."

Needless to say, I was surprised by Richard's comments. He was describing classic symptoms of disengaged users and an inability to effectively drive a strategic system initiative. The repeated financial questions and lackluster user response were also signs of insufficient credibility; exactly the kind of credibility Richard needed to effectively lead this complex implementation.

Richard was right to be concerned that his stakeholders were not responding appropriately given the nature and importance of the project. But it didn't make sense that he was experiencing these issues. He had great strategic alignment to the company's direction, a solid technical strategy, a good team, and an on-time, on-budget track record to date.

I shared these thoughts with Richard, who agreed that he felt the same way. But since I had to catch a plane back to New York our conversation had to come to an end. So I asked Richard if I could come visit with him in a week or so to continue our chat and perhaps get to the bottom of this.

The follow up

We connected at his office about three weeks later and spent the day together. Our agenda:

1. Meet the project team

2. Review key project materials

3. Review the governance and reporting materials used with the executive steering committee

4. Conduct a few short informal talks with key stakeholders

During the course of the day we focused on investigating the following items:

- Where and how did the IT team interface with their business counterparts?

- In what manner and form did Richard and his key project manager communicate project status (including financial information) to the senior executive steering committee?

- How well did the IT team understand the business processes (today's and tomorrows) that the new system was set to bring to life?

- How similarly did Richard, his project manager and the other key IT leaders see the mission and vision of the project and how close was that vision to the vision expressed by key stakeholders?

After a few hours I was able to confirm Richard's concerns. Things were far from perfect. The business stakeholders liked Richard and his team and they felt comfortable with them on the project. However, they did not accord Richard and his team enough credibility and influence to bring about a full and complete engagement between the business users and the IT team. What's more, a number of the executive steering committee members were bothered by the substantial project costs, how the costs were being managed and what the company would really get for this substantial investment. Finally, these doubts were filtering down to the users on the project which further eroded Richard's credibility. The question was: why was this happening?

By the end of the day we had the answer to what was going on.

The answer

On the surface it looked like they had a very good relationship with their business counterparts. They spent time together. They had detailed meetings and reviews. They went for beers together after work. But in terms of the really important elements required to build credibility and influence, Richard and his team had gaps.

Despite managing and executing the project correctly, Richard and his team lacked a certain connection with their business peers. Simply put, Richard and his team were not "close enough" with their business counterparts to command the needed respect and influence.

I realize that "close enough" is a rather vague term—especially in the context of IT leadership. But I have chosen this term very much on purpose. Partly because I want to consciously avoid using the term "aligned," which is highly overused and which I believe means something else entirely. And partly because I want specifically to call attention to the relationship aspect of the problem faced by Richard and his team, which is at the very core of the problem here.

What Richard and his team were missing, and what is commonly found with highly influential IT leaders is a particular type of closeness that works very well in building credibility and influence. I call it *Business Intimacy.*

What you are shooting for in terms of *Business Intimacy* with your colleagues, peers, and bosses is that they feel, in their gut, that you really get them and their issues; that you really know what is important to them and to their business success. It's about achieving a closeness of mind, perspective, and approach with your colleagues. It's about the synchronicity of action that becomes possible between individuals and groups, when acting from a shared and common perspective and purpose.

Why *Business Intimacy* matters

In order to influence someone you have to know them. More importantly, they have to really feel that you know them and that you genuinely care about them. That's because the most important characteristic of an influential relationship is trust.

In the context of a business relationship, it's a trust that comes from a sincere conviction in the hearts and minds of your colleagues and customers that you are working in their best interest and that you really know what their best interest is.

Think about it on a personal level. Who is likely to have greater influence over you, a trusted advisor who knows you really well, or an expert service provider?

Now here is the critical point: Most IT leaders know this. Most IT leaders know that it's important to build trust with colleagues and customers. The problem is that the vast majority of IT leaders go about it in all the wrong ways.

From arranging meetings titled "Building trust and credibility between IT and Marketing" (for real, I actually saw this presentation) to key account management initiatives, I've seen dozens of bad ideas implemented poorly. What is very rare to see, and what is at the heart of *Secret #3*, is how to actually do it. How to systematically build trust.

The trick, or I should say, the secret, is not to try and make a direct assault on building a relationship of trust. Instead, the focal point of your efforts should be on building *Business Intimacy*. And when you attain *Business Intimacy*, you will be rewarded with trust.

Take a minute and think about this last sentence because this is a very, very powerful idea.

It's powerful because it takes the whole issue of trust-building out of an amorphous values-based realm, and transforms it into a practical agenda that can be followed by any diligent professional. By following the appropriate steps that I am about to share with you, you will quickly be on the road to building *Business Intimacy* with your colleagues.

How influential IT leaders build *Business Intimacy*

Business Intimacy is made up of several components. What they are, how they function, and how you achieve each of them is the essence of *Secret #3*.

These four components, or methods, are arranged in increasing order of how difficult they are to achieve. The very best IT leaders employ all four methods. However, not all are required from day one and not all are required on every issue every day.

1. **Proximal intimacy**

2. **Financial intimacy**

3. **Process intimacy**

4. **Strategic issue intimacy**

I'll review each component and then tie it back to the case of Richard.

1. Proximal intimacy

Proximal intimacy is about physically living in the same space as your colleagues and customers. Frequent in-person contact arising from physical proximity encourages informal interchanges. Water-cooler chats, quick drop-by meetings, impromptu coffee machine exchanges on a key issue, and the list goes on. There is simply no substitute for face-to-face human interaction to create a sense of knowledge about one another.

This is why it is such common practice among highly influential IT leaders to place their people within the customer groups they support. Although it may be less convenient than having everyone together in one place, co-locating helps build familiarity and comfort between the IT team and the user community.

How Proximal intimacy works and why it's so powerful

- **It communicates commitment.** Nothing declares your intention to serve a customer's needs like placing yourself (and your people) into their physical space.

- **It breeds understanding.** When you occupy the same physical space as your customers, you absorb a thousand tiny lessons about their needs, their constraints, their priorities, their values—lessons that would be nearly impossible to obtain through other means.

- **It makes you smarter.** Here's Christopher Barber, CIO of WesCorp: "I have eight business relationship managers, each living with and working closely with his counterpart in a specific business unit. These relationship managers continually update me about what's going on in their client organizations... It really helps to understand the business units we're dealing with."

Back to Richard

Richard had a strong team, but they were all centrally located. They interacted with their business peers almost exclusively in the context of planned meetings and conference calls. And that's just not the same as being in the cube around the corner. Without informal forums for addressing quick and easy questions, they stacked up only to be handled at meetings. Sure emails may have been sent, but that's just not the same thing as a quick question answered in the lunch line and then further explicated over lunch.

The absence of proximal intimacy meant Richard and his team were prevented from getting the rapid feedback they needed, which in turn lead to further problems.

2. Financial intimacy

Financial intimacy is about being completely fluent and transparent with all costs that fall under your budget or for which you are ultimately responsible. Since IT services are consumed by the company as a whole and not just by IT, financial intimacy means having a clear method of cost allocation for all customer groups. It means achieving clarity (for yourself and for your customers) on how IT resources are consumed by each and every group.

We'll talk more about how to formally demonstrate your financial intimacy in *Secret #9*, but for now, the key takeaway is: Being fluent in, and having at the ready, everything pertaining to IT costs is the essence of financial intimacy.

How Financial Intimacy works and why it's so important

First, it's just a fact of corporate life that managers who demonstrate a tight control and understanding of money are respected and appreciated by their bosses. Conversely, managers who shy away from budget specificity, tend to be less respected in the senior executive suite.

Second, nothing says that you deserve trust more than demonstrating very tight financial control and clear cost allocation. Doing so communicates the message that you are responsible, that you understand that business is about money, and that you know how to handle money appropriately. In business, nothing is more important than the money.

Third, with a rock-solid control on costs, your dialogue with business unit leaders changes. You move away from being the guy who talks about IT problems, and instead become a peer who speaks about IT services and their costs. You become a businessperson who speaks in the language of business: money.

Last, and most importantly, a firm understanding and control of all the IT costs will create a change within you. You will start to feel differently about yourself and your degree of control over your area, and in turn you will communicate differently. And this new style of communication, backed up by the appropriate support material, will engender strong feelings of credibility and trust.

Back to Richard

In the initial discussion with Richard about his project, he mentioned that the executives overseeing the project were constantly surprised by the costs of the project and had a tendency to ask the same cost-related questions over and over. What Richard failed to see was that the repeated questions about project costs from the executive team wasn't due to a lack of attention on their part, but rather stemmed from the fact that the project budget was never put to them in a fully transparent and understandable form.

It was a costly project and the degree of transparency Richard provided was simply not enough. He wasn't purposefully hiding anything. At the same time, he wasn't working closely enough with the finance team to ensure there was a comprehensive and detailed cost picture.

3. Process intimacy

Nearly every organization operates via a set of defined processes (or at least strives to). Defined processes are the ways in which things get done. From accounting to manufacturing to marketing and sales, processes are found throughout an organization.

In order for you, as the IT leader, to have a full and complete understanding of your customer's business you have to be an absolute expert on your customer's processes. You have to know them inside and out.

It's not that you need to know your customer's processes in order to check off another box on the *Business Intimacy* checklist. You need to know your customer's processes inside and out in order to effectively implement systems and analytics to support these processes. The fact that it's on the *Business Intimacy* checklist is merely a reflection of its importance.

The difference between process knowledge and process intimacy

There isn't an IT leader in the world that wouldn't agree that you need process intimacy. Most, in fact, would quickly say that they do have process intimacy. My experience observing highly influential IT leaders has shown me the huge difference between what most IT leaders have, which is process knowledge and what they should have,which is process intimacy.

Process knowledge means you have an intellectual awareness and general understanding of the business process. It means, if pushed in a workshop, you could probably articulate the key level I steps in a given business process with perhaps a few of the level II details.

Process intimacy, on the other hand, means you can walk over to a shelf in your office (or to a folder on your computer) and within 5 minutes pull up a detailed process map that has been updated within the last 6 months. What's more, it's likely that it was you or a member of your group that put together the process map; because in most cases the business teams don't care to spend time defining and managing process maps. It's us system guys who need them to really understand the process flow subtleties and special cases so we can properly design the supporting systems. That's what I mean by process intimacy.

How Process Intimacy works and why it's so important

Achieving process intimacy requires a serious commitment on your part. You have to proactively research and document business process. The obvious place to begin is with the process maps you probably already have as part of system documentation. But if you want to follow the example of the most influential IT leaders, you shouldn't stop there. You and your team should establish an on-going discipline and program for documenting, updating and generally maintaining the library of key processes and standard operating procedures (SOPs) for each of your customer groups.

Once you achieve process intimacy (or even when you are substantially on the journey towards it), you can expect to see another change in your relationship with your colleagues and customers. You are likely to find yourself invited to business process review and improvement meetings. After all, you have all the documentation and you can help make the meeting more productive and focused. You come to the meeting with a real value add, a real purpose for being there beyond just being kept in the loop.

By documenting and maintaining the company's key processes you secure for yourself a seat at the table (albeit at the functional level). You don't have to ask for it, it just happens on its own—by virtue of the contribution you make. No special requests required. That's because you have earned the seat based on value and service, not because you occupy a position.

When you commit to building and maintaining this process library, you are not only rewarded with the intrinsic knowledge of how your customers operate (which is very, very important), you also get the appreciation and respect of your user community. That's because as much as they might not like keeping up process and SOP documentation, they recognize it's very important and valuable. What's more, they experience first-hand an important service from IT—a service that isn't necessarily linked to a specific system issue of the moment. And finally, and this is the critical point, they see you and your group as truly intimate with their processes. Not just knowledgeable, but intimate. And that further builds a trust relationship.

Back to Richard again

Let's go back to Richard's complaint that despite great attention and effort paid to design and prototyping solutions, the business always came back with an "out of the blue" revision to the process model or a critical issue that required substantial rework.

Upon closer review during the meetings with his team, we found that in the vast majority of cases what the team saw as "out of the blue" revisions were, in fact, gaps in his group's understanding of the current core business processes and how they were envisioned for the future. It's not that the team didn't have reasonable process knowledge, they did. However, they did not have deep process intimacy.

To be fair, it wasn't only a problem for Richard's team. This was a big and complex project that involved a lot of change to a new business model. The business community was often unclear themselves on just how things ought to work in the new model.

The answer for Richard and his team however, was not to wait for the business community to give them all the answers. They needed to become true process experts in the area of content management and multi-purpose publishing in order to further increase their value (and influence with) their colleagues.

4. **Strategic Issue intimacy**

The final aspect of *Business Intimacy* is strategic issue intimacy.

Strategic issue intimacy is about achieving a familiarity with the critical and strategy-related issues facing your customers, colleagues, and bosses. It's about knowing and understanding the key problems and issues your stakeholders, customers and bosses are facing. Strategic issue intimacy refers to major, business-defining questions like:

- What achievements must your CEO reach in order to meet his commitments to the board?

- How is the new product launch by your biggest competitor affecting your company's market share?

- What will be the impact on profits if your company doesn't bring the planned new products to market in the current budget year?

All of the above examples (taken from actual client situations) are classic strategic issues—big and important problems or goals that occupy your stakeholders, customers, and boss' mind in a significant way. You'll know you have achieved strategic issue intimacy when you are able to answer the famous question: "what's keeping your customers awake at night."

How Strategic Issue Intimacy works and why it's so important

Strategic issue intimacy helps you build influence in several ways:

1. It gives you a set of topics to speak about with your colleagues that are guaranteed to be of interest to them (a useful and important tool for getting your colleagues' attention).

2. It provides a set of beacons or anchors you can use to align various IT initiatives that will resonate with your colleagues.

3. It provides a playing field for new ideas on how IT can best support the business.

4. It helps cast you in a role greater than just the "IT guy."

Strategic issue intimacy is like a bonding agent between you and your colleagues. When you are fully aware of, and in sync with, your colleagues' strategic issues it has a transformative effect on your relationship. It demonstrates to your colleagues that you really know them and you really care about what is important to them.

Process intimacy demonstrates that you know what's going on day-to-day in the nitty gritty operational detail. Strategic issue intimacy shows that you understand the bigger picture, that you are focused on what matters most to your colleagues. Most of all, strategic issue intimacy establishes you as a trusted colleague.

What about Richard?

Although Richard and his team had the project well aligned to the business objectives of his company, they missed (or more accurately stated they were shielded from) the two strategic issues that were really wearing on their colleagues; particularly the senior business people in charge of content and editorial and their direct reports.

While they were very much in favor of embracing the Internet and expanding their publishing base, they were also very worried about two things:

1. How would they retain effective copyright and control over the content once it was broken down and componentized on the web?

2. How would the new model affect the editorial approach and the demands on writers and editors?

These were not just garden-variety change management issues; these were fundamental shifts in a business model and in how people and intellectual property assets were going to be deployed. Naturally, the key business users were very concerned. And since this worry was very much on their minds, it was hard for them to be fully engaged in a program that held so much uncertainty.

When I pointed this out to Richard and his team, they were surprised. In fact, they felt nearly the same way about the uncertainty of the business model and were a bit resentful that the business was somehow expecting them to provide process and systems answers to these questions.

From Richard's point of view, it was up to the business community to figure out the answer to these fundamental questions and to provide him with the answers. To be less than 100% cooperative because he didn't have the answers for them just didn't compute. After all, it was a new business model they were building.

Richard and his team – the epilogue

Over the next six months Richard and his team implemented three major changes as a result of our time together:

First, he moved the core project team into the area where the editorial and content development groups had their primary offices. It took a little time to sort out proper working space and it was a bit uncomfortable, but within a few weeks the team reported a whole new level of engagement with their customers. More importantly, the Senior VP of Content praised Richard at a senior management meeting for sacrificing comfort in order to really get close to his people.

Second, Richard and his project director recast the financial reporting for the project. They sat down with the CFO and the Controller and together worked out a new financial reporting framework. Moreover, they set it up so that the new reporting and cost allocation could be administered and verified by the financial group and would be prepared for the IT project director and Richard to review with the CFO and Controller prior to any steering committee meetings.

The result: With the backing of the CFO and the Controller along with the new reports, all questions about the financial situation of the project went away almost overnight. Sure it took some collaborative work with the finance team, but it was more than worth it.

Third, once Richard's credibility improved from his actions in steps one and two, he decided to address his customers' strategic issues. After careful planning, he presented the very sore open issues regarding the business model at a steering committee meeting. At the meeting he asked that the steering committee recognize how serious these issues were for the company, and explained that special time and energy needed to be devoted by the senior management team to give closure to these issues. Richard further made the point that although investing time to address these issues would cause a delay in the project timeline, it was well worth the investment in time and money.

Here too Richard was successful in getting the attention of his senior management and securing their help to address the business model questions. With his newfound strategic issue intimacy, he was able to point out the need to tackle core strategic concerns. And best of all, Richard and his key senior managers attended all the meetings when the business / process model was fully fleshed out.

An important caveat. The story of Richard and his team is a wonderful example of how *Business Intimacy* can build trust and can help address a problematic project.

Please be aware however, that Richard's rapid results came only because he had quite a solid track record in many other areas of IT service delivery (he excelled at *Secret #1* and *Secret #2* in particular).

Richard was also an excellent communicator and he already enjoyed a fair amount of respect from his peers. As such, he was able to quickly turn things around. For managers that are starting from a less solid foundation, give yourself time to build *Business Intimacy*. It doesn't happen overnight.

PART 2

THE ESSENTIALS OF INFLUENTIAL COMMUNICATIONS

part **2**

Secret #4: Three Communication Traps to Avoid

Secret #5: Say No

Secret #6: Be Skeptical

Secret #7: Practice *Ne-ma-wa-shi*

IT leadership requires a great deal of communication. You are forever briefing someone on something. Sometimes you are promoting a vision. Other times, you need to deliver less than wonderful news about a project gone south, a budget exceeded or a service level unmet.

Part II reveals the secrets that underlie influential communications from the unique perspective of the IT leader. The specific challenges that plague IT leaders in particular and the distinctive communication strategies and tactics to use to more effectively influence your colleagues, peers, customers, stakeholders and boss.

THREE COMMUNICATION TRAPS TO AVOID

"Many attempts to communicate are nullified by saying too much."

Robert Greenleaf

It probably doesn't come as much of a surprise to anyone reading this book that IT leaders are, generally speaking, not considered the best communicators. In fact, most IT leaders don't think of themselves as good communicators either. That's unfortunate, because effective communications are both a big part of IT leadership and an essential ingredient required to build and wield influence.

Why it's so tough for IT leaders to communicate effectively

The truth is that most people, not just IT leaders, aren't very good communicators. What's interesting about the communication challenges faced by IT leaders is that to a large extent they can be traced to who we are as people, how we think and how we approach problems.

It's not just IT leaders who suffer from this. If you observe executives from different functions (say marketing and operations, for example) you will begin to notice that certain communication patterns and mistakes tend to be repeated, depending on the communicator's role in the company.

Finance people tend to make their communications too numbers-oriented. They often neglect—or completely leave out—the story behind the numbers. In a similar vein, marketing folks often get so caught up in telling a story and showing pretty pictures that it can be hard to find the bottom line numbers in their communications.

As IT leaders we are obviously not immune to our own set of challenges or traps that tend to stem directly from the kinds of people we are and the type of work we do. These inherent communication challenges often correlate to our role, function and personal orientation. The secret is to know what those specific communications traps are and how to avoid them.

Because of the nature of these traps, if you get caught in them, they not only hamper your communications, they tend to significantly degrade your influence. (You'll understand why shortly.) Avoiding them is therefore critical to delivering influential communications.

The three communication traps

1. The techno-functional trap

2. The style trap

3. The solution-seeker trap

1. The techno-functional trap

In the mid 90's the firm I worked for was hired to help a division of United Technologies with a large-scale upgrade to their accounts payable system using SAP software. David T., the very capable head of A/P systems, was our direct client on the project.

As was typically my job, I spent time with David reviewing the business case, validating the strategic alignment, pressure testing the project plan, and planning out the change management communications for the program. Everything looked to me to be in really good shape. David had worked closely with the A/P group and with SAP to clearly define the project, set out the scope and present the budget and business case. We were all set to go.

About four weeks into the project, just before the contracts with SAP were about to be signed, David learned that instead of the software and services costs from SAP coming in at $6 million (as originally planned) they would instead be about $7.5 million. Naturally, David was very unhappy with the situation. However, given his close relationship with the business user community, he felt strongly that he could go to them, review what had taken place and that together they would work through the budget problem.

Since the project was all set to go, David was eager to resolve this problem as quickly as possible, so he called a meeting for the next day with the business area leadership. David invited me to the meeting (as I had become a pretty common fixture on the team), but I was unable to attend that specific meeting due to a prior personal commitment. However, before I left that day, I suggested to David that he prepare a set of solid justifications for approving the additional dollars.

David felt strongly that the business community knew exactly why they were doing this project and that although they would be annoyed by the extra cost, it wouldn't change the fundamentals. He did however, promise me that he would prepare a few key points just to remind the users of why the project was being undertaken and its intended benefits.

When I reconnected with David two days later, he looked miserable. I didn't really have to ask because the answer was written all over his face, but good manners required that I fake it a bit. "David, how did the meeting with the user community go regarding the budget issue?," I asked.

David responded: "Horrible, simply horrible. I feel like we've been set back six months. It was as if they had all forgotten why this project was being done in the first place. I was on the witness stand having to justify their project. And no matter what I said they didn't seem at all convinced. I couldn't believe these were the same people I built all this rapport with over the last six months."

After a few deep breaths, I gently asked David if he had prepared that set of reminders that I suggested to him when we were last together. "Yes," he said, "and they didn't help a bit."

I asked David if I could see the material he used, so I could get a sense of what he presented and we could get on the same page about what went wrong.

Leaving aside the introductory slides and other non-essential materials, David's reminders about the underlying need for the new system (and the foundation of the case to push on despite the cost increase) were as follows:

1. We need to come up to industry best practices in terms of our purchasing process, throughput times and the software we use.

2. The new functionality will help us a great deal. Our entire purchasing and A/P team will be much more productive.

3. The new system will enable us to clean up our database of vendors and streamline vendor management.

4. By upgrading to the new system, we'll achieve software consistency—the same version of the software across all modules.

After reading David's reminder list, I knew exactly what was going on. David had fallen into the techno-functional communication trap. At a time when he needed to exercise influence over his colleagues, he slipped into a communication pattern that diminished rather than increased his influence.

All of the reasons David provided for the project were 100% correct. But, and it's a big but, they were largely technical and functional in nature. When things were calm and everyone was on the same page, these technical and functional justifications were acceptable shorthand between David and the business users. But once the budget issue popped up, it returned the business users back to the early days of project justification. And what they wanted was reassurance and confidence in the project in the terms they understood—not in David's terms.

It's likely that David's attempts to remind them of the technical and functional benefits of the new system not only went unheard, they probably created further doubt in their minds as they listened for solid business reasons for their investment and instead heard technical and functional justifications.

Why this happens

As IT professionals, we think in terms of technology and functionality; it's the very essence of how we see systems. What's more, it seems perfectly natural to communicate about systems issues in technical and functional terms. And that's why the techno-functional communications trap is the one that most often catches IT leaders—especially when communicating with non-IT colleagues.

Even though you are talking about systems and systems-related issues, when you're seeking to influence others, it is absolutely essential to speak in the language and terms that are meaningful to the other person. To business people, technical and functional justifications are often meaningless.

Revisiting David's justifications

It didn't take long to explain this point to David. He already knew it in his gut; he was just under pressure and rushed things a bit. Together we sat down and re-crafted the key justifications for the A/P system upgrade. Here's what they read like when we were done:

- The new purchasing system is set to shrink the average time it takes to process a PO from three weeks to six days.

- The new system will reduce the cost of our PO administration from $383 per PO to $312 per PO.

- The new system will enable us to take advantage of the quick pay discount offered by 30% of our suppliers yielding a potential savings of up to $90 million.

- The new system will qualify the purchasing and A/P departments for the six sigma bonus being offered by corporate.

See the difference? These arguments are all about what's in it for them—in the terms and language that is meaningful to the business users.

But notice: To speak this way, you must think this way. You must gather information with these thoughts in mind: What's in it for them? How can I translate the technical or functional benefits that I see into tangible language that means something to the other person?

The lesson here is fundamental: Avoid your natural tendency to communicate in technical and functional terms. It's your job to translate your functional and technical insights into terms that speak to your audience.

2. The style trap

Closely related to the techno-functional trap, yet still distinctive in nature is the style trap. WesCorp SVP and CIO Chris Barber puts it this way:

> "There's no universal way you can treat people and be effective. Some people, they just want the skinny: "Tell me what it is and we're done." Others like to talk about their kids—they like the chit chat, the small talk. Some people take direction verbally, but with others, I have to make a visual presentation to them because they're very visual people. It all depends on the individual. Some people like you to be very direct with them; others like a little bit of finessing. Some people require a lot of handholding. The point is, you have to be able to evaluate the individual and what they need to be effective when you're communicating to them."

Many IT leaders assume that others think the way they do. They believe that other people process new information in the same manner, style and with the same personal predispositions that they do, particularly as it relates to IT projects.

When they communicate, these leaders act as though others share their mental attitude, mental framework, and emotional constitution. Big mistake. Because it's much harder to influence someone when you are communicating in a style and manner that is foreign to them. They are often so busy trying to figure out your approach, that they aren't really hearing you. And you certainly won't be able to influence them.

Highly influential IT leaders, on the other hand, invest a great deal of time and energy understanding their own personal style and learning about the styles of their colleagues, peers, customers and boss. They then make a special effort to modify the style of their communications according to the style of their audience.

Justin F., the VP of application development at a Fortune 100 pharmaceutical company, was particularly good at not only avoiding this trap, but in turning his audiences style preferences to his advantage. He was keenly aware of the preference of the CEO of the company for one page summaries. No matter what the topic, the CEO believed it could be summarized into one page. So regardless of the topic or its complexity, Justin worked and worked until he had it down to a one pager.

When he would present to the CEO or the executive committee (all of whom quickly adopted the CEO's one-page preference) Justin would always begin by handing out his one page summary. Then, after quickly reviewing the key points on the summary page, he would proceed on to a more substantial set of slides that he would use to give more detailed explanations and to answer questions.

In my opinion, it was Justin's adaptation to the CEO's style that was a major contributing factor to the very strong budget and moral support he received from the CEO and the other senior executives. Yes, he had very sound plans, but so do many other IT leaders. Justin's however, rarely met with significant resistance. When he spoke, he was listened to carefully. He had real and meaningful influence by virtue of carefully adapting his communications style to that of his audience.

How to avoid the style trap

Fortunately, awareness of this issue is pretty high across corporate HR and training departments. After all, it applies not only to IT professionals but to all people. Many companies have pre-approved training programs like Myers Briggs or the DISC assessment that will help you learn about, and better identify the appropriate communication style for your target audience. These programs help you understand your communication style within the context of all of the basic communication styles. The good ones will also teach you how to identify someone else's style and how best to communicate with people of different style types.

If you are fortunate enough to work for a company that has this sort of training available, I encourage you to embrace it. Typically, you undergo a self-assessment exercise, followed by an explanation regarding your style and the style of others.

Once you have completed the training and you feel somewhat comfortable with these new insights, ask your colleagues for their help in implementing what you have learned. You will be surprised how many of them will happily share with you their style and joke about the best way to communicate with them. This is extremely valuable information for improving your influencing capability with them.

Mark O'Gara, VP of Infrastructure Management at Highmark, summarized the benefits of style awareness as follows:

> "Our ability to influence the organization was greatly enhanced just by understanding the precise composition of the leadership team—their personal styles and preferences."

3. The solution-seeker trap

The last trap is a particularly nasty one for IT professionals and it's the least obvious of the three. That's because on the surface it doesn't look like a trap at all. Quite the contrary, it looks like just what every IT professional ought to be doing. And that's why it's a secret!

We've gone solution crazy

As IT professionals we are trained to be "solution-oriented" and that's a good thing. We are expected to deliver solutions to our customer's business problems leveraging the power of information technology. The problem is that the industry as a whole has become solution obsessed.

Over the last 20 years, tech vendors of all types have shifted away from selling products and services. Instead, everybody now sells a "solution." Everywhere you look: Storage solutions, security management solutions, revenue leakage solutions, product lifecycle management solutions, and the list goes on and on.

The solution-based paradigm is helpful in addressing a specific and clearly delineated problem area. With pre-built features and functionality that match up to the requirements of a known problem area, a pre-packaged solution can be a great timesaver.

However, this solution orientation also creates a tendency to quickly sort problems into pre-existing solution areas. It creates a bias towards listening to a problem only for as long as is necessary to determine into which solution area it falls.

Today's typical IT professional is looking for the quick fix, a 70%-80% off-the-shelf solution in order to quickly meet the needs of his customer.

So what's the problem?

The challenge is that in our desire to identify a good solution we often do not take the time to carefully listen, hear and fully understand **all** of the problem. And that is the solution-seeker trap. In our desire to come up with solution, we unwittingly cut our listening short.

We are so focused on quickly reaching a solution that we often don't get a chance to really hear and understand the full problem. The minute we see a problem or set of problems that line up with a known solution area, we make a beeline for that solution area. We shift out of listening mode and into solution adaptation mode. As our clients speak about their needs, we are already thinking about how we are going to implement them in a particular package.

Unfortunately, in terms of our ability to effectively influence, this impulse can be counterproductive because it leaves our customers and colleagues with the feeling (albeit subconsciously) that they were not fully heard. That's a shame for our customers and a real influence killer for us. Because even though you think you are giving your customer exactly what they are asking for, i.e., a quick solution, in the back of their minds, they don't really feel heard.

Making things worse, we have trained our customers and colleagues to think in nearly the same way. Our colleagues and customers no longer come to us to discuss a business problem. Rather they come to discuss packages and solutions. And naturally, wanting to be customer oriented—we follow along.

Avoiding the solution-seeker trap

In order for your customers and colleagues to feel heard—and for you to really get to the bottom of their issues—you have to take the time to really listen to their problems, to hear the full back story. Most of all, you will need to listen long enough to ask the right questions.

Listening is a two-fold skill, a matter of both:

1. **Not talking**—letting the other person have the floor, take center-stage; completely surrendering your time and attention to the other person's thoughts, feelings, desires, goals, views, and

2. **Asking the right questions**—probing, drawing out of the person what's really going on, his or her views, and real concerns.

Learning to listen can be difficult, but if you are open to it and you are open to asking real probing questions and then hearing the answers it will have a transformative effect on your communications. That's because you will be shifting your communications from being purely utilitarian in nature to more personal in nature. Personal relationships call for genuine, human, sympathetic listening with a view toward understanding the other person's perspectives, both business and personal.

As IT professionals, with a strong systems and solution focus, we sometimes forget there's a person on the other side of this business relationship, not just a project or problem to solve. We don't listen long enough or ask nearly enough questions to get down to this person's genuine motivations, issues, and concerns. It seems counter-intuitive, but the more questions you ask, the more you bypass the quick fix and put the brakes on the march to an immediate solution, the more likely the person you are talking to will feel truly heard. And when you do this an important opportunity will open up for you: The other person will say something along the lines of, "So what do you think?"

At that point you'll have their full attention. At that point you will be really well-positioned to effectively exercise your influence.

Bottom Line: Avoid these three traps by applying the strategies and tactics we have discussed in this chapter and your communications will *automatically* become more influential.

SAY NO

"Given how often I have to say "no" to people around here, I'm expecting to be fired any day. I just want to make it easy to go when that day finally comes."

Walter Peltz, CIO (former)
Medco

I'll never forget the moment when I heard that from Walter. It was maybe the first or second time I ever met him. I was escorted into his office and the very first thing I noticed was how empty it was. Almost no books on the shelves, no pictures, no decorative ornaments. The desk was nearly completely clean. It looked and felt like an unoccupied office.

After the usual introductions, I casually asked, "is this a new office for you? Did your group recently move?" That's when Walter answered me the line that I have quoted above.

At first I thought it was a joke. So I chuckled and then looked at him expecting him to continue on with the "real" answer. But Walter just sat there, deadpan. Then in a very matter-of-fact way he said: "It's good not to have too many personal things around that make you feel tied to the place. It's work." It was clear he meant exactly what he said.

It was one of those big "aha" moments you get in your professional career – a moment of total clarity. I was already a believer in not taking on more than could really be done. I understood the importance of standing firm on scope and expectation management. (I learned that the hard way from over-committing to clients and getting burned). I had observed successful IT leaders push back on their colleagues who came with wish lists and project demands that didn't make sense for the business. But I never quite heard it said like this. And I certainly never saw anyone internalize this discipline and approach to such a degree that they would ready themselves for dismissal at a moments notice.

From that day on, I became very conscious about this issue of saying no. I watched how and when IT leaders said no. I observed the effect of saying no in place of yes. I watched the careers of IT leaders who more frequently said no as opposed to yes and vice versa. And what I found really surprised me. The IT leaders who said no more often were the ones who enjoyed greater respect, status, budget and pay.

I'll get back to Walter later on in the chapter, but for now let's turn our attention to the essence of this secret, why it's so important and how it works to help you build influence.

How "no" got such a bad reputation in IT

Over the last 20 years IT has moved from the basement to the front office. This transition (which is still going on) has not been smooth. Most of today's IT leaders have been part of this shift and have very clear memories of the not-so-good old days. In particular, IT leaders remember how often they had to say no to their colleagues requests (or tell them it would take a very long time), because of inherent limitations and difficulties in yesterday's systems. The result: IT became the butt of many jokes. We were thought of as unresponsive at best, at times even incompetent. Just saying the words "ask IT for that change" had people rolling their eyes with that knowing look of "forget about that ever happening soon." As much as IT leaders wanted to be responsive to their colleagues requests, their hands were tied given the state of technology at the time.

Naturally, this didn't leave IT leaders with a particularly good feeling about themselves, their group or their ability to bring value to their company. After all, nobody likes to say no. Nobody likes to be thought of as the "bad guy," the one who has to deliver the bad news all of the time. And as much as you might explain the reasons for the "no," it's still not a fun place to be, no matter how you cut it.

As the PC revolution gave way to client server computing and finally to web computing of today, it brought with it sea changes in what could be done in much shorter time frames. And now, emboldened by new tools and technologies and a desire to repair the reputation of the past, many IT leaders have moved to "yes" as the default answer for project requests. And that's where the trouble began.

A perfect storm

In addition to the desire to repair the stigma of the past, three other factors have come together to create a perfect storm for IT leaders.

1. The shift to a customer-oriented mindset and model

2. The pressure from external vendors

3. The illusion of quick and cheap

1. The shift to a customer-oriented mindset and model

As IT groups began to grow in size, scope and importance, IT leaders started to rethink how best to organize and deliver service. Within a short period of time, most IT departments began referring to their business counterparts and colleagues as customers or clients.

What makes this mindset and approach problematic is that the word customer or client conjures up very specific attitudes and behaviors on the part of the service provider. The famous motto "the customer is always right" may be appropriate in a purely commercial relationship, but it's not always appropriate in a peer relationship.

This customer orientation has even lead some IT organizations to talk in terms of "selling" projects to their clients. They have literally come to the point where they believe it is their mission to go out and "sell" different types of projects to their "customers." The thinking: the more projects they do, the more valuable their business peers think they are. Wrong.

But wait, there's more.

2. The pressure from external vendors

In the not-so-good old days, new business systems, of any type, could only be deployed with the direct and substantial involvement of IT. With the advent of client-server and then web computing all that has changed. Targeted functional solutions running on departmental servers, on outsourced platforms, or on a software as a service (SaaS) platform have sprung up everywhere.

IT is no longer required to bring these solutions to life. Solution vendors, thinking of their bottom line, take their wares straight to the end users of the system —bypassing IT altogether. Then, through first-rate salesmanship and a stream of demos, the vendors successfully convince the users to either deploy their systems on their own, on an outsourced platform or "force" IT to join the party and implement it with them in house.

Caught in a sea of increased activity and escalating requests, many IT leaders seem to have lost sight of their roles as managers and stewards of technology. They can't bear the thought of going back to being the bad guys saying no, or the idea that the technology might get away from them. So instead, they took on the role of service provider to all (backed up, of course, by their favorite consulting firms eager to help them do the work).

I can't even begin to count the number of times I have had the following conversation.

Me: "Why are you doing this project? It doesn't fit in with your plans or architecture at all."

IT Leader: "We have no choice. If we don't do it, the business will just go out and hire a vendor directly and do it themselves."

Sound familiar? Now, for the last element.

3. The illusion of quick and cheap

Last, but certainly not least, is the illusion that solutions can be deployed quickly and cheaply. While it's true that many of the costs associated with technology deployment have come down, there is no such thing as quick and cheap; no matter what the vendor tells you.

True, with today's platforms and services it is much easier to be up and running with a very basic, non-customized solution to many business problems. But the real work of making the system truly reflect the needs of your organization takes time, effort, focus and money. Unfortunately, the pressure from the market, combined with a desire to shed the "no" reputation of yester-year and become more customer-oriented, has caused many IT leaders to forget this. And that's how the scourge of saying yes to way too many requests occurred.

The result

Too many IT leaders feel compelled to say yes to nearly every project request; some even actively sell new projects to their colleagues. The result: reduced credibility and diminished influence.

How you see yourself

This secret goes beyond saying no as opposed to saying yes per se. It cuts to the core of how an IT leader needs to view his job and role and in turn conduct himself. On the one hand, there is the mentality of a responsive service provider who tries to always say yes to his customers so they will like him and continue to use him. (Read as: keep my job, in this context).

On the other hand, there is the mentality of a seasoned executive who recognizes the very difficult job he has as the steward of the technology platforms, choices and investments of his company. This executive accepts and even welcomes the healthy conflicts that arise in evaluating every technology-related investment against the appropriate business and technical criteria. Most importantly, this executive embraces his critical role and unique ability to set and adhere to a technology strategy that truly serves the business needs of his company, not the momentary desires and ideas that may arise in one department or another.

Back to Walter

And that brings us back to Walter Peltz of Medco, who as you can imagine was never fired from Medco, but rather retired after a long and very distinguished career. Walter did not say no just to be difficult; he said no because his best business and technical judgment told him to say no. Bear in mind, Medco's business is processing pharmacy claims and providing drugs via mail order. Their systems handle over $50 billion worth of claims for tens of millions of Americans using tens of thousands of different pharmacies, health plans and doctors. In essence

Medco is one huge computer system. So the fact that Walter was able to hold the line and say no in an environment that was so computing-intensive is further proof still of the importance of learning how to say no.

But the most interesting aspect of Walter saying no at Medco is not so much the many "nos" but one very significant "yes." Early on, Walter and his team made a strategic investment in data warehousing technology. They reasoned that given the nature of their business and the constant demand for information from customers, researchers, and other business partners the company would best be served by deploying a data warehouse.

Walter and his team went on to invest tens of millions of dollars over many years in building and fortifying this data warehouse. It became well known throughout the IT industry as one of the largest data warehouses ever built (second only to Walmart). More importantly, this data warehouse forms the backbone of Medco's rapid reporting and analysis to customers, a service that has consistently helped place Medco's offerings ahead of its rivals. This strategic advantage, and the funds necessary to maintain it, was made possible by the many nos to the other projects that would not deliver. And this brings me to the final point of this chapter.

When you are known as a thoughtful IT leader, one who is willing to fight the good fight and say no to projects that should not be done (for whatever reason), then when the time comes and you do say yes and you do advocate for a project to be done, your yes and your recommendation carry much more weight and influence. And that's the essence of this secret.

BE SKEPTICAL

> *"The beginning of wisdom is found in doubting; by doubting we come to the question, and by seeking we may come upon the truth."*
>
> Pierre Abelard

A surprising attitude and approach wins the day

Secret #6 is all about attitude, approach and demeanor in IT-related communications. And I have to admit, that as an IT professional and management consultant this secret really surprised me as I observed it over the years.

You see, I am a pretty high-energy, positive thinking and optimistic sort of person; and I bring this attitude to work with me every day. And like most people, I believed that my attitude and approach to IT projects worked best. Heck, what client wouldn't respond to my positive and optimistic energy about the promise of information technology and how to make it work for their organization? Well, turned out I was wrong.

After working with a number of very successful CIOs and being told to dampen my enthusiasm a bit, I started to notice a pattern. The prevailing attitude and approach to IT projects most commonly employed by highly influential IT leaders was one of balanced skepticism. Not cynicism or harsh skepticism, but balanced skepticism.

These IT leaders approached IT projects with a pretty skeptical view of every claim made by the project team. They questioned the benefits promised, the maturity of the solution, the reputation of the vendor, the change readiness of the company and so on. And even when re-assured by their team that matters were well in hand, they continued to doubt until they saw the new system up and running, the users working properly, and their organization benefiting from the solution as promised.

The ultimate success story

Although I observed this attitude and approach in many successful IT leaders, no story so fully encompasses this secret, and illustrates its power and reach as the story of Partner Communications, a $2.5 billion cellular communications and content company.

In September 1999 shortly before the company's IPO on NASDAQ, the CEO was traveling the world doing roadshows for potential investors. In less than 2 years, the company had gone from startup phase to the fastest growing cellular provider in its market. And despite highly competitive market forces and established players, Partner was taking away market share from its competitors at an incredible pace. (Fast forward to today and Partner is the #1 cellular provider in its market by every measure.) Anyhow, back to our story.

During one of the CEO's early presentations he was asked by some of the analysts to explain the secret of the company's sales and marketing success in such a short period of time. He began by crediting the sales and marketing teams for their efforts, but then he said something completely unexpected.

> " …what makes our marketing work so well is the very powerful data warehouse and analytics program we have. We have invested heavily in the technology and systems to understand our customers and marketplace. As a result we are able to design marketing campaigns and service programs that appeal to our target customers."

It's not very often that a CEO makes specific mention of a technology initiative as part of the company's competitive advantage in the marketplace in such a critical public forum. If ever there was a demonstration of the strategic value of technology and the clear recognition of it's importance, this has to be one of the best examples of all time.

At the time, I was a practice leader with PricewaterhouseCoopers and my data warehousing team was working closely with the IT team at Partner. It was an incredible shot in the arm for us all and served to further reinforce our commitment to this project and client.

Before I tell you exactly how this story relates to the point on skepticism, allow me a brief moment of personal gratitude.

Over my 25+ year career in IT-related management consulting and systems implementation, I have had the privilege to work for dozens of the world's leading companies on three continents. I have enjoyed working with many fine companies and individuals and have seen many success stories (and a few not so successful stories as well, I'm afraid). However, I have to say that the Partner data warehouse program occupies a unique place for me. It was a shining example of how to really do it all right. How to truly leverage the power of information to achieve competitive advantage.

Sure my team worked hard, but the real credit for the success of this program goes to the incredible IT leaders at the time, particularly: CIO, Sami Keinan, Chief Architect, David Margalit and Data Warehouse Program Leaders, David Shalev and then Limor Malay.

OK, a little background and then back to skepticism.

Discovering the power of skepticism at Partner Communications

It all began in 1997 when Partner Communications was nothing more than a joint-venture investment company with a skeleton staff of 25 people set on acquiring the rights to operate a third cellular phone company in Israel. In April 1998, the Ministry of Communications awarded the rights to Partner for a fee of approximately $400 million. Additionally, the ministry specified in its award that Partner had to be up and running with nine months or else begin to pay fines for sitting on the license. It was an unheard-of timetable.

Within days the company went into near 24/7 operations. Sami Keinan, a seasoned IT executive with a strong track record of large-scale systems implementations in the telecommunications industry was recruited to the position of CIO and put in charge of deploying all the business systems necessary to support a company that would shortly have 1,000,000 customers. In other words, no short cuts.

Sami quickly built out his group of senior managers and called in his former colleague from Digital Equipment Corp, David Margalit, to act the chief architect and to oversee the deployment of critical integrative systems such as the data warehouse, middleware and so on.

My firm, PricewaterhouseCoopers, was chosen as the system integrator and consultant to assist Partner with this deployment due to our experience with large-scale telecom data warehousing. It was an important and high-profile engagement for our firm and as the practice leader for this area, I stayed very close to the project. That's how I came to spend a great deal of time with Sami and David.

Setting the tone from early on

From the earliest meetings I had with Sami and David they made it very clear to me that failure was not an option. The company was under very tight timeframes and the IT deployment was a major risk factor. At the same time, they made it clear that the timeframes were not to be used as an excuse for anything less than first-rate implementation quality. I, of course, assured them that our firm would deliver and made my case as to why they should feel confident that we would meet their expectations.

I assured them that with our global reach, we would be able to tap senior staff and experts from other locations and could, at a moment's notice, augment the team with the right people to make sure we met our commitments. It barely moved them. All I got was skepticism and concern. I figured it was natural given the early stage of the project and went to work eager to prove them wrong.

As time went by and the project team achieved its targeted milestones, I expected my conversations with Sami and David to improve. No such luck. The two of them continued to express skepticism about every aspect of the program. They were never cynical, just concerned and skeptical about every date and commitment. And they were eager to hear exactly what we were planning to do to address their skepticism. And this attitude wasn't just vis-à-vis our team, it seemed to extend throughout the enterprise; to every major system deployment.

Even as the project started to meet milestones and deliverables, it didn't seem to change much. After a few months of this treatment on a nearly weekly basis, I started to wonder what was going on. Why wasn't there a change in attitude? Weren't Sami and David excited about the project and its achievements?

Finally, a break in the ice

As the data warehouse went live and started to deliver on the company's expectations, Sami and David opened up a little bit. They were pleased with the accomplishment and became more approachable.

One evening, I sat with them and asked them straight out, why they had been so skeptical about the whole program. Was there something our team didn't do quite right? Something we needed to learn for the next time.

Sami and David explained to me that actually, they were delighted with how the program went.

I was shocked.

I told them that from the on-going skeptical attitude I hardly got that impression. That's when they explained the essence of their approach, how it works, and why it's so important.

Although not their words exactly, the reasoning behind their skeptical attitude was as follows:

A look behind the curtain

First and foremost they explained, a skeptical attitude to IT project outcomes reflects the default mindset scientists bring to every new experiment. Until it is proven to be working, the scientist needs to be skeptical. That's just part of good scientific approach and method.

Beyond adhering to the basic tenets of scientific protocol, adopting a skeptical attitude to IT projects brings several key benefits.

First, it unites the project team "against" the boss who is skeptical of the project. This helps bind them together as unit with a shared desire to show the boss that he is wrong. (This effect is particularly powerful on outside vendors. I can vouch personally for that.)

Second, it helps keep the focus on the key areas of risk that are the cause of the IT leader's skepticism.

Third, it provides a tangible example of the type of attitude and approach we are trying to cultivate in the next generation of managers. If they don't see this approach and attitude in action, how will they learn it?

But the real benefit of being skeptical is the influence it builds for us with our colleagues. By adopting a skeptical approach, we actively adopt the same mindset they have. In a matter of speaking, you might say, we place ourselves alongside our colleagues on their side of the table.

That's it!

The last point made by Sami and David is particularly important and I have had it validated numerous times over the years. Here's how it works:

Most non-IT executives are very concerned about IT projects. They are inherently concerned about the project being successful, especially when their own in-house people are involved. And when you outwardly and vocally adopt a similarly skeptical attitude, it causes them to feel understood and validated.

So often senior executives are promised the world only to be disappointed later on. A skeptical attitude guards vigilantly against this and therefore prevents disappointment. Senior executives really appreciate this.

Your skeptical attitude not only assures them that you are worried about the same things that they are worried about, it frees them from having to grill you on the various risks and concerns they may have regarding the project. That's because they see and hear you bringing it all up on your own.

The net result is that you are seen as a risk-conscious manager, who doesn't get all caught up in the project hype, and who is there to ensure that a steady hand is applied to the running of the project.

Looking back

As I sit here today, I suppose it doesn't come as much of a shock to me. After all, this idea follows on naturally from *Secret #2 (Expect Projects to Fail)*. However, ten years ago it seemed somewhat counter-intuitive. Weren't IT leaders supposed to demonstrate enthusiasm and optimism to their peers in the organization? Well, it turns out that to build influence, a little less enthusiasm and a little more skepticism wins the day.

Please don't confuse the skepticism I'm describing with cynicism, negativism, or a lack of desire to go do things. You have to do things, you have to be responsive, and you certainly cannot be cynical about any project. But you can bring a measured degree of skepticism that is based in the reality of IT projects.

This skepticism needs to be rooted in risk management, a focus on identifying the problems, and retaining the demeanor of a calm, collected executive, not an excited IT cheerleader.

IT leaders have a difficult line to walk. On the one hand, you need to advocate for the appropriate technology investments and need to be able to move the organization forward toward realizing the benefits of information technology. On the other, you have to watch over those very same projects with a skeptical eye. Not an easy task. But that's what it takes to earn the influence you need.

SECRET #7

PRACTICE NE-MA-WA-SHI

"It's easier when the customer is standing up at the table with you, talking about what they need and how IT can help. That way it's not IT trying to negotiate dollars on its own; we're doing it with the customer and that's a much easier conversation."

Ben Berry, CIO
Oregon Department of Transportation

Nemawashi is a Japanese agricultural term. It means: "going around the roots" or "smooth the roots before planting." It's a statement of wisdom directed at farmers when transplanting a tree. It instructs them to take special care and ensure that the roots of the tree are accepted into the soil. This statement, which has made its way into mainstream business vernacular in Japan, has come to mean much more than that in modern Japan.

I first heard the term Nemawashi in 1997 while consulting to Matsushita Electric Corporation (owner of the brand name, Panasonic). At that time my firm, PricewaterhouseCoopers, was helping develop and deploy a large-scale analytics and information system that was likely to expose managers in the company to new ways of thinking, many of which would challenge their old ways of thinking and managing.

Several months into the project, I was working hard on envisioning all the analytics, getting everything ready to present to the upcoming meeting of the senior leadership steering committee.

Before that big meeting, I decided to run my ideas by one of the Japanese vice presidents who was a proponent of the project and understood its importance. I was eager to get his approval.

I showed him all the new reports and my vision for the project. When my presentation was finished he turned to me and said, "The reports and analysis are good Marc, but what about the nemawashi?"—I had no idea what he meant, but I soon found out.

He explained that my desire to present at the upcoming meeting just a week away was unrealistic. He said we needed at least several weeks so we could meet individually with all the key stakeholders and talk to them about the vision for the new system. He said we had to go over all the reports and the analysis with them, ensuring that they understood how the system would work and giving each the opportunity to add his own stamp to the presentation. He said it was important that the presentation reflect their ideas, not just mine.

I was quick to point out to the VP that indeed I had visited with many managers and executives and heard their point of view. That I had spent a great deal of time carefully listening to everyone's needs and perspective and that the material he had before him already reflected that reality.

The VP smiled at me with the knowing look of the elder statesman about to school the new foreign service recruit in the basics of diplomacy. He folded his hands and began.

> "Of course you spent time with our managers and executives. That is how you were able to learn enough to put together this material. And that was a very important exercise. But this is still only your synthesized impression of what was said to you combined with what your professional experience tells you we need.
>
> We are very grateful for your hard work and experience. However, it is now time for each of our key managers and executives to encounter the compiled material privately and to react to it in its new form before they have to comment on it or approve it publicly.
>
> The nemawashi process is not about convincing everyone that your vision is correct. It is about getting the benefit of everyone's input in a manner that is safest for everyone to tell you the truth and to be helpful to you.

It is also about helping our managers and executives become comfortable with new ideas so they do not feel ambushed on the day of the big presentation; particularly if some of the material being presented threatens them in some way.

The nemawashi process will not only help us accept the new reports, it will help our people learn to trust you, because they will see that you are actively working to avoid causing them any embarrassment.

And last, nemawashi will not only help our people feel part of the process, and enhance their acceptance of the change, it will help you learn more about your own ideas, enabling you to improve them."

Gulp!

There really wasn't much for me to say after that except thank you. And off I went on my first real journey of nemawashi.

I was aware of what pre-selling before a big meeting was all about (that's what I was doing with the VP), but he challenged me to do something quite different. He challenged me to really connect with and listen to my clients. He challenged me to slow down and focus on the real communication needs of people.

What happened

So I made a little change. In place of trying to sell my ideas to the client, I adopted a different posture as I went back to meet with the key managers and executives. I took the advice of the VP to heart and went asking questions, seeking guidance, looking to improve on the early ideas for the new reports and analysis. (In fact, that was the name I gave to the presentation material I used during my first nemawashi process: "New Reports and Analysis - Early Ideas.")

It was during this process that I experienced the power of this secret, the power of practicing nemawashi, for the first time. Because the more I stayed open to the feedback and critique of the Panasonic managers and executives, the more we were able to improve the materials. The more I listened and genuinely tried to act upon their ideas (even if I thought I knew better), the more receptive the client became to my ideas. The less sure I was of my ideas and their value and relevance, the more open, appreciative and influence-prone the client was. It seemed to work almost in reverse. Less selling and promoting of my ideas lead to more acceptance of those very ideas. I simply couldn't believe how much more genuine influence this approach delivered. What's more, the final product improved substantially from the input I received.

At first I thought that it was a cultural thing. That it was a uniquely Japanese business practice. So I tried it out on another client who was implementing a CRM system a few months later.

Sure enough, it worked in nearly the same way. Magic. (OK, maybe not magic because it does require some serious work, but incredible nonetheless.)

And that's the secret of "Practice Ne-ma-wa-shi"—it works across all cultures and industries. Since then, I've personally practiced nemawashi in the US, Asia and Europe and it has worked every time.

The nemawashi challenge for IT leaders

I've shared the above story and my approach to nemawashi with many IT managers over the years. In almost every case the initial reaction I receive is similar to my own of years ago. Typically people say, "Oh, I know what you're talking about, you mean pre-selling."

In case I wasn't clear enough in the preceding paragraphs, permit me to emphatically restate that **nemawashi is not about pre-selling**. The two differ in very important ways. Pre-selling is a valid process in the context of closing a sale. It sets up the sale with the customer by delivering an initial sales message prior to the formal sales pitch.

The idea is that by pre-selling, the customer is gently initiated into the sales process. They hear the key messages and any initial objections can be dealt with. Then, when the customer is exposed to the full sales pitch, they are more receptive to it. With pre-selling you have a product or service to sell and you are looking for the very best way to make that happen.

The nemawashi process is not about handling objections and setting up "the close." Nemawashi is about sharing ideas, building a joint understanding, demonstrating respect and openness, and harnessing the power of the collective.

At it's core, nemawashi recognizes our fundamental human nature as it pertains to group discussions and decision making. Nearly all people feel uncomfortable making decisions or being challenged in public forums. Nemawashi provides a process for key discussions and decisions to be reviewed and generally agreed upon privately, beforehand. Nemawashi allows for this process of pre-agreement to occur naturally. As people participate and feel heard, achieving buy-in and acceptance of the final product occurs almost reflexively.

Socializing ideas – nemawashi by another name

Former CIO of Worldspan, Sue Powers, uses nemawashi to encourage her colleagues to consider a new IT system or business process, she just happens to call it "socializing an idea."

In an article in CIO Australia, Powers explained that socializing means "active engagement and interaction outside formal meetings, where people are less guarded." According to Powers, people are more likely to openly discuss change during casual conversations in the hallway, at the water cooler, in their offices, or over lunch. And, she says, because they're more likely to discuss their objections, finding a solution is easier. "In a formal setting," she writes, "people can feel pushed into an idea. This way they feel they can be more honest."

Advanced nemawashi – share the credit publicly

When you take the time to get your colleagues ideas about improving your plan, strategy (or whatever the item may be) you acquire a powerful weapon to earning their support. But the very best practitioners of nemawashi don't stop there. To further build their rapport and influence with their colleagues when the day of the big presentation comes they work hard to make other people the heroes and make their ideas shine.

Highly influential IT leaders give public credit and thanks to their colleagues for their specific contributions on an initiative. They take special care to point out the detailed contributions made by their colleagues, not just some general statement of thanks. When presenting an idea that came out of the nemawashi process, they describe it as their colleague's brainchild—even if it was mostly their idea that was only modified slightly by their colleague.

This public recognition goes a long way to strengthening your relationships and it solidifies your colleagues support for your program, with which they are now publicly identified.

PART 3

PART 3

GAME TIME

Secret #8:　You Gotta Know the Game

Secret #9:　Your Three Signature Plays

Secret #10:　Get Your Team to Really Play

Secret #11:　Take Your Game on the Road

Armed with the right kind of credibility and the essential communication tools, you are ready to step up to the plate and interact with your colleagues, peers, customers, stakeholders and boss in a new manner.

Part III explains the game you will be playing and what you need to do to excel at the game.

YOU GOTTA KNOW THE GAME

"Understanding the subtleties of our business and how it compares to others in our industry has been a great help to me—the unique things that we do to move our business forward as opposed to our competition—that's what's really important to know."

Akhil Tripathi, Senior Vice President and CIO
Harleysville Mutual Insurance

You gotta understand the business!

In the IT world, we've been hearing this call, this commandment, to IT leaders for as long as I can remember. But despite constant repetition, it still seems to be a chronic problem for many IT leaders. A personal experience may be useful for illustrating the point.

I spend a great deal of time helping senior IT leaders and their business colleagues envision the strategic application of technology to their business. As part of this activity I supply my clients with a pre-consult checklist. It's a simple list of materials I ask clients to assemble for me, so that I can learn as much as possible about them, their organization and their industry before our in-person meeting.

The list of requested materials varies based on the nature of the work, but almost always includes several pretty obvious items. Typically these include:

- An industry overview (as seen by their company)

- The company mission and vision statements

- Current business strategy

- A description of their strategic advantage(s) in the marketplace or their Unique Sales Proposition (USP)

- IT strategy

- IT organization mode

- IT service delivery model

- IT service scorecard

Does it surprise you to learn that less than 10% have ever sent me all the materials prior to our meeting? 75% provide me with nearly nothing at all.

In some cases, the IT leaders simply don't have access to the materials. In others, they claim that such materials don't quite exist. In the majority of cases I hear, "It's all pretty much up in the air right now and that's why we want to speak with you."

The reasons however, don't really matter. The net result is still the same.

In company after company, before I ever have an opportunity to talk about technology-based opportunities or strategies (as planned), I spend a great deal of time teasing out of the IT leaders AND their business colleagues the essential information about their business required to gain a real understanding of their company and their unique situation.

At first I thought it was just my clients that were challenged in this way. Over time, I learned that this is a widespread and very common situation. So I looked into it more carefully.

What's going on

What I found was that nearly all IT leaders know they need to understand the business. That's beyond obvious. However what they don't quite understand is exactly what that means. In fact, the vast majority of IT leaders interpret the phrase "understand the business" to mean: understand the priorities, needs, wants and requirements of the business area for which they are responsible.

And while this is not wrong, it is not a deep enough understanding of the business for achieving and maintaining boardroom-level presence. And it certainly isn't a sufficient level of understanding to effectively support you in your attempts to influence board-level executives.

This brings me to the obvious question and the essence of *Secret #8*: What then exactly does it mean to "understand the business"?

What are those special things that IT leaders need to know about their business in order to be able to really play at the most senior levels?

Secret #8 answers these important questions. It explains the table-stakes knowledge and information you need to have at the ready in order to effectively play in the influence game.

The three dimensions of business understanding

A business (like any organizational unit) is a complex web of people, processes, ideas, history, money and so much more. It's therefore helpful to have a method for getting our arms around it. I use a method called the three dimensions of business understanding.

These three dimensions don't so much break down and categorize the business— a simple functional model can do that. It's more that they tell the inside story of the business. They expose the essence of the business and what makes it unique. The three dimensions of business understanding are:

1.   The business/profit model

2.   The operating model of the business

3.   The competitive position

1. The business/profit model

The business/profit model highlights the key profit drivers for the company. It provides insight into the relationship between revenues and costs, how they relate in terms of the company's operations, and ultimately what products and services are most profitable. It highlights cost advantages and disadvantages. Multiple companies may operate in the same general market space, but their specific business model and profit drivers differ substantially.

A good example of this is the big box retail business. At first glance companies like Costco and Walmart look similar. But a closer look reveals very different profit models. Walmart drives profit with its unique sourcing and supply chain model.

Costco has a completely different model. They sacrifice nearly all profit on the items they sell in order to attract and retain members. It is the fees they charge their approximately 60 million members that make up the lion's share of their profit.

Not surprisingly, the IT investments at each company reflect the differences in the core business model. Costco has huge IT investments in its customer databases and membership management systems. Walmart on the other hand has world-class supply chain and logistics management systems. Similar variations in the profit and business model can be found in many other industries as well.

Capturing the attention of the executive suite

One story that illustrates the power of business model knowledge and how it can be put to use by IT leaders comes from my early days applying these ideas on behalf of IT leaders and their teams.

At the time my client was a company called Learning International, one of the leading providers of sales training in the world and a subsidiary of Times Mirror. I was working with the IT team lead by Margaret DeMartino and her two key senior directors, Dave Harrington and Steve Notchik. Together we were building a new IT strategy and plan.

During the strategy formulation and presentation process, Margaret, Dave and Steve had some early successes reframing IT with the senior executives and they started to enjoy more attention from and influence with the senior leadership team.

Just as the IT strategy formulation was coming to an end, the CEO of the company at the time called Margaret with a request. He shared with her that the company was planning on making a strategic acquisition of a sales force automation software company. He explained to Margaret that for some time the company had been looking into purchasing a software company because of the potential to expand their offerings and enshrine their award-winning sales training into a software tool. The executive team reasoned that with Learning International's customer footprint they could quickly ramp up sales of the software product to both existing and new customers; something that would take any software company on its own much, much longer to do—if they could even do it at all. All this made sense to Margaret and she asked how she could be helpful.

The CEO explained that they had identified one company in particular based on a number of business, financial and marketing criteria. However, before he went ahead with the deal he wanted Margaret and her team to have a look at the company and the product as well and to evaluate it from an IT perspective.

[A quick side note: Margaret, Dave and Steve were able to quickly increase their profile and influence with their senior management because they were (and still are) first-class professionals and managers. What's more, they had a crack IT group with extremely well-run infrastructure systems and applications which gave them a great deal of credibility as per Part I of this book. In *Secret #9* You will learn how they handled the strategy presentation process.] Now, back to the story.

Margaret was, of course, pleased to be involved with this sort of a strategic initiative and was keen to do the best job possible. It was my good fortune to be working with her at the time, and since I had spent a great deal of time in the SFA and CRM area, Margaret asked me to help her and her team with this evaluation.

After a few quick conversations with the marketing and sales teams, it was pretty clear that the business folks really liked this company. They loved the look and feel of the software and already had clear ideas about how to marry Learning International's content with the software tool. Marketing already had some preliminary sales estimates based on a variety of promotion strategies to their existing customer base and felt that this software would make a big difference to the company's growth over the next few years. Net, net—a lot of people wanted this deal.

With this as a backdrop, we prepared a number of questions for the software company's executives. Margaret and her team held a number of conference calls and I went to meet with the development team of the company for an in-depth, behind-the-scenes look at the product and the support infrastructure.

It didn't take long for us to figure out that while this company's products did indeed have a wonderful look and feel, this was the result of substantial customization done on a client-by-client basis. And although the product looked similar on the front-end, in fact there were at least a dozen or more substantially different versions of the software. It's not that the business folks were completely blind to this, it's just that the seller's agents *spun* this as a wonderful advantage of this company—that it was flexible and adaptable to different client situations.

Now this isn't necessarily a problem in and of itself. Many software companies thrive using this model, where they create highly customized versions of their software for clients and then maintain and enhance those versions over time. But it did present a problem for Learning International.

When we regrouped to discuss how to present our findings to the CEO, the team put forth the following basic memo as a starting point.

Version #1

To: **CEO**

From: **LI - IT Leadership Team**

Subject: **IT Due Diligence review of SFA Software Vendor**

Following a careful review by the internal IT group of Learning International and supported by external experts in the field of SFA software, we recommend against moving forward with the acquisition due to the following weaknesses in the product:

- Lack of a solid core product
- Multiple code bases installed at different clients
- Varied support model and costs by customer type
- Substantial effort required to customize software

In short, we do not believe that the amount of money and time required to make this software work for our company's needs merits the investment. Further details supporting our findings and conclusions can be found in the attached reference pages.

On the surface this memo seems perfect. It's short, to the point and very specific. And the content is 100% correct. But given the strong positive predisposition to the company by other groups within LI, we needed to find common ground with the business folks in order to effectively influence them. And that's when we turned to the business/profit model for help. Using the business model as our anchor, we re-drafted the memo as follows on the next page:

Version #2

To: **CEO**
From: **LI - IT Leadership Team**
Subject: **IT Due Diligence review of SFA Software Vendor**

The good

There are a number of very positive aspects to this product and company. The product is well-suited to our methodology. The interface and user experience are crisp. The basic technology platform being used is sound. The development and support teams are competent. Most importantly, the company has happy customers and is profitable.

The challenge

The underlying business model at this software company varies substantially from ours.

How is this the case?

LI model. Our business model is built upon standardized product offerings, rapid rollout and low-cost service requirements. We have a mature product line with well-defined modules. Our training materials are completely standardized and 85% of our customers use them as is. This model enables us to serve large numbers of customers in a cost-effective manner. It also enables us to maintain a competitive price point in the marketplace.

Software company model. They don't really have a core product. Although there are a set of standard modules, they exist in name only.

The lion's share of their money comes from customized implementations followed by highly customized service and support.

There are a dozen plus different versions of the software deployed at different customers. Each customer's implementation and service is configured and priced differently in order to correspond to the customer's unique needs.

Bottom line

Their product and business model could be brought into line with ours, but that will take time and money. We are likely to pay far less and to undertake far less risk just hiring this company to build us a product than if we purchase the company outright.

You see the difference? In the first version we emphasized the key facts. In the second version we emphasized the mismatch between the business models. Needless to say, the executive committee was very impressed with the team's findings. But more than that, the fact that the IT group connected with their colleagues around the business model further enhanced their standing and influence with the executive leadership.

2. The operating model

Closely related to the basic business and profit model is the operating model. The operating model is first and foremost the living, breathing, working instantiation of the business / profit model we just covered. But your company's operating model is more than just that. The operating model encompasses your company's philosophy, approach, and methods of operation. Finally, the operating model expresses how your organization uniquely gets things done.

I first learned how important it is for IT leadership to understand the operating model about fifteen years ago from John Craparo, then an IT leader at GE Capital. (Today he's a senior VP at HP.)

At the time John was considering our firm to help support a large-scale technology upgrade for a few of GE Capital's large business units. As we worked through the business case together, I tried to impress upon John the potential value of upgrading the smaller business units at the same time as opposed to doing just the large ones. I demonstrated to John that the savings associated with a wider upgrade would be substantial and could easily save GE Capital $2 to $3 million on the project.

John listened carefully and considered my arguments. Then he told me that although there may be potential savings he was going to stick with just doing the big units for now. He then made the critical point when he said: "To risk possibly disrupting the operations and activities in some of the smaller business units was contrary to the philosophy and operating model of GE Capital."

I was puzzled.

GE Capital was known as a tight-fisted, money-conscious organization. I was sure John (and by extension GE Capital) would welcome the opportunity to save money. I wondered what was the big deal in including a few of the smaller business units in a large-scale technology upgrade. It was at that point that John "schooled" me in the philosophy and operating model of GE Capital at the time.

John started off by explaining to me how GE insiders referred to different business units within GE Capital. It went something like this:

Within GE Capital, you were not given the distinction of a "business"—you were not accorded legitimacy as a genuine operating division and unit—until you reached $100 million in profits. (That's right, $100 million in *profits*.) Until then, you were a venture. And in the GE Capital world, ventures were meant to be totally unencumbered, given maximum flexibility. Saving $1 million or $2 million through a corporate initiative, which was relevant to a mature business—one with profits in excess of $100 million—did not make sense for the smaller venture groups.

Even though there may have been absolute savings for GE Capital as a whole, these savings did not merit moving away from GE Capital's basic operating model. Upgrading the smaller units alongside the bigger ones would have meant getting the smaller units to fall in line and comply with corporate IT policies regarding the upgrade. This was viewed as potentially interfereing with GE Capital's operating model which called for fierce independence for its ventures. The company treasured that model and was keen on preserving it.

It was a lesson I never forgot. It taught me how powerful a force an operating model can be. It can even be more important than short-term, quick monetary gains (in theory the greatest benefit an IT solution could hope to deliver).

This story really opened my eyes to how important it is for IT leaders to be deeply aware of the subtleties of their company's operating model. All too often when applying IT solutions or IT thinking, IT leaders are so focused on meeting specific business objectives or delivering ROI that they inadvertently place themselves at odds with the basic operating model of their company.

A company's operating model is often the result of years of expensive trial and error. It evolves to offer the company the best opportunity for success. Trying to deploy IT solutions in a manner that isn't fully in sync with the operating model not only sets you up for failure, it's bound to diminish your influence in the company. Such an approach will only demonstrate to your colleagues and customers that clearly you don't get it. Or put another way: *You don't understand the business.*

In the GE Capital example, understanding the business didn't mean knowing this group finances large equipment purchases, or that group runs credit card operations for big retailers—not even close. It meant understanding, as John did, that saving a few million dollars through a large-scale, multi-divisional, corporate initiative was at odds with the basic operating model of GE Capital at the time.

In subsequent years I've bumped into this issue many times. I've seen—

- CIOs out to do leading-edge, highly aggressive initiatives, but at companies whose fundamental operating models were slow and conservative;

- CIOs eager to save money through centralized technology, but in companies determined to preserve divisional freedom and distributed decision-making;

- CIOs eager to enshrine knowledge in process and systems, but in companies whose operating models focused on strengthening people and relationships.

In all of these cases the motivations were good, but what killed the influence of these IT leaders wasn't their personalities, their presentations or even the validity of their plans. It was the fundamental mismatch between the operating model and philosophy of their company and that of the project.

3. Competitive position

The final dimension of business understanding is competitive positioning. Competitive positioning describes how your company is uniquely equipped and configured to sell and service customers as opposed to its competitors.

To have a comprehensive understanding of your competitive positioning you will need:

- A solid awareness of your industry, including how you fit in with upstream suppliers and downstream customers

- An in-depth understanding of your competitors products/services and how exactly they compare to yours; where they are strong and where they are weak

- A realistic and fact-based SWOT (strength, weakness, opportunity & threat) analysis of your company and its key products and services

- A clear understanding of the strategic advantage or unique competitive position your company currently enjoys or is pursuing with respect to its competitors

- A list of the forces that are most likely to impact your unique competitive position in the short and long term

What you are looking for is a clear picture of the key pieces that need to fall into place for your company to be successful today and into the future.

Note - Obviously I don't expect you to come up with all this information on your own. You should get it from the marketing and sales teams. It's their job to actually create it. It's your job to *know* it.

So where is IT on this?

Business is a highly competitive game. Sales reps live and die by it. Marketers stake their reputation on understanding it, finance feels it, and the CEO loses sleep every night because of it. But—and it pains me to say this—many IT leaders I've met over the years don't fully appreciate the competitive nature of their businesses. They don't fully understand the dynamics of the industry of which they are a part. Although many have a pretty good handle on the business and operating model, they often aren't fully aware of how their company measures up to the competition generally, and in the eyes of their customers. These same IT leaders, by the way, do think they understand the business. But in reality, they only understand the most recently introduced business objectives or tactical programs that they are focused on supporting with a new systems initiative.

Please don't make the mistake of confusing a thorough and comprehensive understanding of your competitive position with knowledge of your company's key objectives and programs. The former is a pre-requisite to influential interactions with your peers; the latter—just the talk of the day.

Another personal experience: I've spent many years working in the pharmaceutical industry, where brands are the lifeblood of the company's existence. I've attended many meetings where well-meaning and dedicated IT folks were discussing the systems initiatives they wanted to present to support a particular brand. For example: at one company the IT folks knew of a brand's desire to get more involved in consumer marketing and had a host of possible solutions to present. During our meetings, I asked what the competing brands were doing. My question was met with blank stares. Unfortunately, this was hardly an isolated case. In many similar meetings, the IT folks knew little about the brands against whom they were competing and were often unaware of their company's relative positions against those brands.

Of course this is not the case with all IT leaders, particularly not the highly influential ones. This is one area where influential IT leaders really set themselves apart from others. They make sure to keep fully abreast of the company's competitive position at all times. They know how critical this knowledge is for building *Business Intimacy* (see *Secret #3*) and for effectively engaging with the customer-facing groups within their organization.

Writing to her peers in CIO.com, Michelle McKenna, at the time senior vice president and CIO of Universal Orlando Resort made this point:

> "Any CIO can take a few steps to get market savvy. We get weekly data about what happened in the park and what the spending trends are per guest. CIOs need to get copied on reports like that and then to study them and look for patterns. Don't be afraid to ask questions about it; give yourself permission to be a smart (and inquisitive) businessperson."

A special nod to customer experience

Every day your customers "experience" your company via technical solutions and platforms—whether it's through e-commerce, auto-fulfillment systems, call center systems, sales force automation systems, marketing automation systems, or invoicing and financial management systems. Each of these systems has the opportunity to positively or negatively affect your company's competitive positioning.

I'm happy to say that many IT leaders (especially the influential ones) are not only aware of this but are very sensitive to the potential strategic advantage the customer experience can have for the company. Of all the aspects of competitive positioning, it's the one area where I have found many IT leaders have unique contributions to make. As commerce becomes more digitally driven, the ability to fully understand and identify with your customer's experience as they interface and interact with your company is of increasing importance. The almost natural orientation to this area is an asset IT leaders should exploit when thinking about supporting the company's competitive vision.

During our research process we encountered many examples of IT leaders investing time and effort in understanding not just the digital but the personal aspects of customer experience. Two noteworthy examples:

> "I spent the first three to six months visiting lots of agencies, spending time in their offices understanding how they conduct their businesses, what they thought about our products and our technology capabilities—all so I could focus on how to use technology to move forward for Harleysville."
>
> — Akhil Tripathi, CIO, Harleysville Insurance

"When I first came to Marshfield, they were looking for someone to be responsible for our reference laboratory business. They wanted a pathologist, not to sit in an office and interpret tests, but to actually get out and be a resource for the clients who actually used our laboratories. So they literally gave me a set of car keys and said, 'go out and make this successful'. So here I was, an MD with a board-certified pathology background, and I'm basically acting as a salesperson. And it changed my perspective, because I had an outside view looking in."

— Bob Carlson, CIO, Marshfield Clinic

Why these three dimensions are so important?

From M&A activity to operating systems upgrades, knowledge of your organization's business model, operating model and competitive positioning sets you up to deal with the senior leadership of your organization as a peer that is in touch with the most important aspects of the business. Knowledge of these three dimensions takes you beyond a basic understanding of business operations and into the heart of the organization's being.

With a command of these three dimensions of business understanding you put yourself in the best possible position to influence your peers and bosses, because you will be speaking from the same perspective as them. (At times you may even be the one that reminds your colleagues of what the business is all about, as in Margaret's case.)

But beyond the broad and overarching benefits you enjoy from the three dimensions of business understanding, there are a number of specific tactical benefits you will quickly see in your journey to acquire and effectively wield more influence. They are:

- **Budget requests become easier.** In a world of competition for budget dollars, your knowledge of these areas will: (a) give you foresight into how your budget requests are likely to be viewed, and (b) focus your budget requests around those areas that directly support the business model, are in sync with the operating model and further the company's competitive position. And when you do that—both in working with your peers to formulate the request and then during the actual budget request process— you not only attract positive attention and respect, you position your requests for approval.

- **Projects naturally align with the business.** With clarity into the three dimensions, you will naturally begin to question every project in terms of its alignment with one or more of these dimensions. This will likely lead to you requiring every project to more specifically and clearly demonstrate how it supports the competitive positioning of the company, and /or strengthens the business and operating model. The result: a natural move toward closer alignment with the business objectives. No need for special committees, meetings, or task forces. Just good old fashioned IT leadership putting the three dimensions to work and following the obvious questions that arise.

- **You are listened to more.** When your subject of conversation revolves around the three dimensions and their manifestations, you automatically attract more interest. That's because this is what is of interest to the other senior managers of your company. And when you are able to talk about this material in a fluid and natural manner, it demonstrates that you are a true peer.

- **It sets you up to move into the next level.** Relating to your peers and bosses in these terms will provide you the opportunity to: (a) demonstrate that you should be given admission to their decision-making forums, and (b) meaningfully influence these folks once you get there.

Competitive positioning – the most relevant dimension for you

Your company's business model, and operating model are indeed the core dimensions of business understanding and it is absolutely critical for you to be fully fluent in your company's business and operating model (more on why in the next chapter). But it's likely that it will be your knowledge of competitive positioning (and ability to apply it) that is most often called upon as an IT leader.

That's because your company's business and operating model are so core to its existence they are unlikely to be changing very quickly. As such, the number of issues that may clash with these models is relatively small. However, in the fast-moving world of business today, companies are constantly shifting their competitive positioning. Moreover, large companies (those with multiple products or product areas) often have a variety of competitive positions based upon the specific product.

Finally, competitive positioning is likely to feature heavily for you as an IT leader, because so many of the strategic and tactical programs and systems you are asked to implement are justified by virtue of the competitive positioning they support.

So what's the message here?

Basically, do whatever it takes to get a solid hold on your company's business model, operating model and competitive positioning. Read all of your company's financial statements and filings. Get copies of all of your operational and analytical reports. Read trade journals, websites and analyst reports. Attend industry conferences. Join peer groups. Ask questions. Know your business and operating model cold. And finally, become a devoted follower of your company's competitive positioning. It is likely to feature prominently in your influence-seeking interactions.

With your newly acquired knowledge of the three dimensions of business understanding in hand, you are ready to put them to work in *Secret #9*.

YOUR THREE SIGNATURE PLAYS

"You can't just walk into a boardroom with a vision."

Thomas Flanagan, CIO
Amgen

Signature plays—athletes and teams have them. An athlete's or team's signature play(s) are the ones that score the goals. The ones where they shine brightest; where everyone (both on the field and off) says: "that's cool."

But what exactly does the term mean in the context of IT leadership? How does it apply to you as an IT leader?

In the realm of IT leaders working to gain access to the executive suite, *Your Three Signature Plays* are the plays that give you a "seat at the table."

From defense to offense

Until now we have essentially been playing defense. By this I mean that The Secrets we have covered so far have stressed largely defensive moves that help build influence. Moves like: how to build the right knowledge about your business; how to identify and avoid common traps; and how to approach communications and project oversight.

These moves are important to use so you don't accidentally rob yourself of the opportunity to gain influence. They focus on the essential elements of credibility and communications as it relates to readying yourself for a more influential role in your organization.

But how do you get that influential role? How do you really capture the attention of your company's senior management?

It's one thing to play a defensive game—training in the business, avoiding mistakes, and reacting to what comes your way in the most influence-building way possible. It's much tougher to proactively go and out and build your influence, to set up a play and step into the game. So, how do you get out there and get noticed without acting like a self-promoting jerk?

That's the essence of *Secret #9*. And that's what the three signature plays are.

Your three signature plays are your offensive moves. They are the three key moves you have as an IT leader to get noticed, be appreciated, demonstrate value and secure your place at the executive table.

These moves command executive attention. They are the moves that highly influential IT leaders play again and again in order to capture, hold on to, and increase their influence.

How I first discovered the three signature plays

Interestingly, I learned the key offensive plays for the IT leader not from an IT leader at all, but rather from a highly seasoned, energetic and well respected marketing executive Terry Augenbraun. I met Terry when he was serving as a senior vice-president of marketing at Chesebrough-Ponds, the consumer packaged goods (CPG) company and maker of such famous brands as Ponds Cold Cream and Ragu sauces (now part of Unilever).

Terry was (and still is) a very high-energy CPG marketing expert. He grew up in the trenches of Playtex and Maybelline and he has been the creative force behind dozens of cosmetics and fragrance brands including some of today's biggest celebrity brands.

I had the good fortune to work with Terry early on in my professional career. It was the early days of database marketing and I was very focused on building expertise in this area. I had some early success applying database technologies and analytical algorithms to sales and marketing problems within small and medium-sized companies, and I was keen to take these ideas to larger companies. Working with Terry was my first opportunity to take my ideas to the "big leagues."

Terry was intrigued by the ideas and results I shared with him regarding the insights into consumer and channel behavior that could be achieved by integrating data from a variety of secondary sources. He was particularly interested in combining data on sales trends, sell-through, and consumer demographics in order to better plan and target his campaigns. (Today that sounds rather obvious, but we are talking about nearly 25 years ago.)

I was hired to help him understand and identify the data integration opportunities. Then, once the opportunities were identified, he would pass them on to his IT team to implement. And since I was working for Terry (as opposed to IT) I had the opportunity to really see things from the marketing perspective.

Not surprisingly, Terry's desires from the IT team far outstripped his budget or the IT team's ability to deliver effectively. And although they had the best intentions, the IT team just couldn't seem to effectively face-off with Terry. This often left Terry (and everyone else present) pretty frustrated before, during and after our meetings.

One day, after a particularly unsuccessful meeting with the IT director—who was both trying to explain why Terry's wishes were unrealistic and at the same time convince him that IT's proposed workaround would give him exactly what he wanted—the whole project nearly came undone. Terry, who is a classic CMO, just looked at the IT director and said, "I am trying my best to understand you, but frankly I have no idea what you are talking about." (It's a line I have heard many, many times from marketing executives when referring to IT). In desperation the IT director answered, "Never mind, it probably wouldn't work anyway."

Shortly after the IT director left the room, before I even had a chance to start translating for Terry what had just happened and what the IT director was really trying to say, Terry turned to me and said something very much like this:

> "You know Marc, these guys want to help. I can tell. But they just can't get out of their own way. I know they want to do the right thing for the company and they want to support me but honestly, I don't think they get it at all.

> I'll give you a perfect example: In addition to these delightful meetings regarding the database initiative that you attend, I get pretty regular requests to meet with them. At first I was more open to meeting with the IT folks, but now I have very little time for them. They are just all over the place.

One time it's to interview me for a new system they want to build. The next time it's an invitation to see a vendor's software solution to some marketing-related problem; or so they think. And then on other occasions they want to meet to discuss my budget for them. I just have no sense of how all their "stuff" fits together and how it all matters to me."

At that point I stopped Terry and asked him: "OK then, leaving aside the current project, what would you like to hear from the IT director? What are you interested in meeting with him about?"

Without missing a beat, Terry jumped up from behind the round side table in his office where we were sitting (he doesn't like working behind a big desk), and in a highly animated fashion said:

"That's easy. There are three things that I want from my IT leader.

First, I want him to have good control over all the IT-related costs we incur. And I want him to be able to show them to me in a way that matches up with my budget. I don't want to have to chase him for the up-to-date numbers and allocations. I want him to be on top of all the numbers so the CFO doesn't come whack me with some unexpected IT allocation charge at the end of the quarter. I want him to really worry about every penny of mine that is flowing through his hands.

Second, I want my IT guy to really know what's going on outside of these four walls. I want him to know what our competitors are doing with technology and I want him to know what's working and what's not. I want him to know where technology is heading. And I want him to have some sort of vision for how we ought to be using technology.

Third, I want my IT guy to have a basic strategy and plan for achieving that vision.

And last, but certainly not least, I want my IT guy to make sure that everything we talk about or do with IT fits into one of those three areas and I am able to clearly see it.

It's really pretty simple stuff, not particularly technical in nature, just simple business stuff. I just never seem to get it."

That's it. That's the moment when I first learned the secret to playing offense.

In his frustration, Terry laid out for me exactly what he, as the senior marketing executive, wanted to hear from IT. What he was truly interested in meeting about. In the simplest terms possible, he explained exactly what it is that really commands the attention of senior executives; even the attention of a high-energy, creative, senior vice president of marketing at a top-flight, fast-moving consumer goods company.

It was a very important "aha!" moment. No more guessing what might interest the CMO; no more selling ideas; no grasping at projects that may or may not get his attention. I had the answer straight from the horse's mouth, exactly what he was interested in hearing and learning about from IT.

1. That the IT leader has firm control and understanding of the state of his finances and costs vis-a-vis IT. That's what I have come to call **the control play.**

2. That the IT leader has a vision—**the vision play.**

3. That the IT leader has a strategy and plan for moving towards the vision—**the strategy play.**

That's how I started to develop the three signature plays. And although these plays have undergone refinement over the years, they still remain remarkably close to their original incarnation.

Each of these plays addresses critical requirements of the business. At the same time, just running these plays, i.e., stepping up to the challenge of these plays and proactively delivering them, not only positions you for more influence, but places you into the key executive management forums within your organization.

Over the last 20+ years I have helped senior IT leaders build and deliver one or more of these plays hundreds of times. Never, and I mean never, did the IT leaders who worked these plays meet with a lack of interest. That's not to say that every play was an immediate and huge success. Some were out-of-the-park home runs, some were just singles. But at the very least the plays delivered on their most important purpose: they provided access and a platform for influence. They began a process of taking your game to your colleagues as opposed to just waiting in a reactive mode.

Aim for the sky

The very "gutsy" objective of the three signature plays is to get you a seat at the table. That's right. Here is where you go for what you really want. But we don't just wake up one day and announce that we want a seat at the table. It simply doesn't work like that. Nobody wants to be on the receiving end of that play. So here is how you start.

Putting the plays to work

The three signature plays are distinct in nature. They are, however, configured to work together in a particular sequence that achieves maximum impact. That sequence is first the control play, then the vision play, and finally the strategy play.

Why this order? In short, the control play establishes your credibility and business presence with your key stakeholders. It provides you with the right audience and positioning. The vision play, the real lynchpin of the three, capitalizes on that audience, takes your position to a new level and sets you up for the big move. The strategy play follows through on the momentum put in place by the vision play and puts you firmly at the executive level.

This particular order of execution is important, because (1) It follows the natural business management rhythm and cycle, and (2) It provides the best opportunity for implementing the ideas behind *Business Intimacy* taught in *Secret #3* and the principles of nemawashi as reviewed in *Secret #7*. But beyond the conceptual reasons for this order is some cold hard experience.

In my consulting work over the last 15 years, I have helped many IT leaders work on all three plays. Not surprisingly, the most frequently requested area of assistance has been IT strategy. Many times I have tried to work directly on the strategy play in a stand-alone manner. Occasionally it has worked out fine to start right in with the strategy. However, in the vast majority of cases, it was impossible to go straight for the strategy. There were just too many missing pieces of knowledge on the control and vision side. This was also usually accompanied by too narrow a relationship with the stakeholders to support presenting an IT strategy right away.

Net, net—follow the sequence here. It's been proven many times over.

What exactly is this "play" thing? How and where do I use it?

Essentially a play is nothing more than a discussion with one or more people supported by some highly targeted presentation material.

Sometimes you will be making your play in front of a large audience, like your entire IT group or at a company meeting. At other times, you will be making your play at the water cooler or over a beer at a company off-site event. Sometimes your play will be in response to a request from elsewhere in your organization. But the real purpose and value of the three signatures plays is that you can and should initiate them on your own. You should use them to go on the offensive.

The three signature plays are built to easily fit into your existing management environment and for some of you the forums and presentation opportunities to which I will shortly refer may already be in place. If that's the case for you, consider yourself lucky. For those of you that still have to establish the forums, don't sweat it. The plays have built into them a natural progression to "next steps" which invites the setting up of the next forum. And once you start delivering the control play a new dialogue will begin with your stakeholders. A dialogue that will bring new opportunities to deploy the vision play and eventually the strategy play as well.

PLAY BY PLAY REVIEW

The Control Play

The essence of this play is a demonstration of your complete and total control of all that takes place in IT from a cost and quantitative performance perspective. The objectives:

1. Shift your dialogue with your peers off of projects and systems and on to dollars and cents

2. Be seen as a strong business executive not just the IT guy/gal

To initiate this play, you will create and deliver a set of monthly and/or quarterly reviews of the IT-related services provided to and consumed by each of the various business units or functions in your organization. These reviews come in two forms. The first form you should call the *IT Business Review*. It should be prepared for each functional area or business unit you support with that unit as the main focal point. In addition to the data about the particular functional area or business unit, it MUST include comparisons to other functional areas in the company. (Nothing gets a senior executive's attention like being compared to his peers.)

The second form should be called the *IT Flash Financial Update*. It should contain nearly the same information as the *IT Business Review*, except that it will not have any particular business or functional unit as its focus. Instead it will present an aggregate and comparative analysis between the units. This review should be prepared for and reviewed with the CFO, controller and your boss.

Both of these reviews will be all about money and metrics. They will set out in the most clear and tangible terms all the key financial and operational parameters relating to the provision of IT services: costs, service levels, delivery metrics and so on. This is **not**, I repeat **not** a qualitative review of the projects. This is purely a quantitative review accompanied by the appropriate qualitative analysis of the numbers.

When you prepare the materials to support this play, bear in mind the following questions. These are the questions that will be in the mind of your audience (even if it's only subconsciously). And for the play to work, you have to ask and answer these questions for them:

1. How much does IT cost me?

2. What do I get for my money?

3. Where do I stand relative to total budget?

4. How is my IT cost allocation applied? What percentage goes to infrastructure, what percentage to support, application development, and so on?

5. How do my costs and what I receive for them compare with my peers in the company?

6. How do my costs compare broadly within the industry?

7. How is IT performing for me and my people? How does it compare to their performance for other groups in the company?

Preparing, discussing, debating, revising and eventually settling into a pattern of simply going through this highly quantitative review *is* the control play. Providing this information and analysis on a regular basis demonstrates that you are a seasoned manager with the ability and confidence to transparently present what is going on.

For many of you, the meetings required to deliver this play will either replace or lend substantially clearer focus to existing meetings. For those of you that do not have meetings like this already on the calendar, be bold. Just set one up. You can have great confidence that your senior managers are just like all the other ones in the world. Which means that if you have any meaningful IT spend at all, they will welcome this sort of review process.

Delivering the control play and engaging with your colleagues, customers, peers and bosses using very focused business performance metrics and dollars will have a powerful impact on your relationship with them. It will set you up as a businessperson that carefully watches the money and what they get for it. It will likely take a few months to get this review on to solid ground and for your customers/colleagues to understand and accept all the numbers. Once they do, it's time to move on to the vision play.

The Vision Play

Once the regular *IT Business Review* meetings are going well, it will create an atmosphere that is conducive for you bring up additional topics for discussion; and that's how you introduce the vision play. You will "steal" some time from the standard agenda and add a new item for discussion. That item will essentially introduce the topic of your IT vision.

Please note: Do not, I repeat, do not call your agenda item IT Vision for XYZ Company. That's an almost guaranteed way to kill it. Perhaps further down the road you can use the "vision" term, but for now, stay away from it.

What I have found works pretty well in nearly every industry, is to label the agenda item, and the discussion in general, "technology-based challenges and opportunities." As you move forward with the process, a more specific title, one that calls attention to the key changes in your particular industry will develop. For example, with clients in the pharmaceutical industry I have successfully used the title: "Digital Healthcare and the Pharmaceutical Industry - Opportunities and Challenges." Of course you don't need to use this exact phrasing, just make sure to avoid using the terms IT vision until others start using it first.

OK, back to executing the vision play.

Obviously, you aren't going to move to this play unless you are properly prepared, so I'm going to assume you have done your homework as per *Secret #3 (Business Intimacy)* and *Secret #8 (Know the Game)*, and that you do in fact have some very interesting and thought-provoking ideas regarding what's happening in the world of IT and how it may affect your industry and company. With those thought-provoking ideas in hand, you are ready to get into vision formulation and presentation.

As explained in *Secret #7 (Practice Nemawashi)*, you are unlikely to have much success presenting an IT vision if you bring a totally finished product out of left field. Accordingly, your first step will be to introduce one or two of the key technology-based challenges or opportunities you see on the horizon—along with an analysis of how this issue may be of importance—to the particular functional area head with whom you are meeting. And then you will ask a simple open-ended question: "What do you think about this?"

This will begin your discussion about key developments in the world of IT and their possible impact on your company. Voila, you have launched the vision play.

Clearly, the vision play doesn't end with one open-ended question. Quite the contrary, it is just the beginning. But before I describe how the vision play is meant to unfold, let's quickly go over the objectives of the play so you understand what you are shooting for in this and subsequent discussions.

The vision play has a number of objectives:

1. To demonstrate that you bring a unique and meaningful perspective on the world of IT and how it is likely to affect your industry in general and your company in particular.

2. To demonstrate your ability to strategically connect IT with your company's business.

3. To build understanding, respect and consensus with regard to your vision.

4. To introduce (and promote) the idea that an IT landscape review and vision should be a permanent input into the company's overall strategic planning process.

5. To rally the IT team behind a coherent vision they can be proud of.

As you can see, there is a lot going on with this play. That's why it's so important to do your homework and get this one right. And it's equally important to allow it to unfold gradually. What that means is that you can't expect to walk into the boardroom one day and present your vision. You have to let it build slowly over time.

You start by sharing a few ideas with each of the business unit/functional leaders in your monthly business review meetings. You will come back several more times to discuss similar items, all the while focused on having a real strategic dialogue and demonstrating your intimate knowledge of your company, industry and the world of technology as it uniquely applies to your company (as described by Terry.)

At first you'll keep the meetings small to make sure you have good traction, agreement and joint ownership around key ideas. Then, as this topic takes up more time and interest with your colleagues, you will suggest creating a separate meeting forum to fully and properly review the overall IT landscape. To this meeting you will invite all of your key customers, stakeholders and boss. And that's when you make the BIG vision play, when you present the full picture of your vision of IT, and the opportunities and challenges it presents for your company. By this point all of the attendees have heard their own part of the vision so you will be presenting to a friendly and supportive audience. This makes a big difference.

Now here's the really important part: At the end of your vision presentation you include a section called "Next Steps." And in the "Next Steps" section you write: Review strategic options and responses. That's how you set up the strategy play. In other words, you leave your audience hanging. You present your vision and the identified challenges and opportunities, but you do not give them the final answer—i.e., what they should do about all of these challenges and opportunities. You leave that answer for the next meeting, because the answer to that question is the core of your strategy and needs to be delivered in the strategy play. (No, it's not sneaky. It's just effective storytelling and staged information delivery management. Marketing and sales do it every day of the week.)

A final reminder before we move to the strategy play. The essence of the vision play (as I learned from Terry and many others after him) is to demonstrate that you can bring some real perspective to the executive discussion table. Talking about the benefits of a single global instance of SAP won't cut it. Vision—and by extension, strategy—require you to step out of the confines of your environment and actually see what's happening more broadly. It means you have to help your colleagues make sense of what's taking place out in the world of technology, both generally and within your industry. And finally, it means you have to translate those trends into concrete challenges and opportunities for your company.

The Strategy Play

OK, you have arrived. You now have a seat at the table. On the strength of the challenges and opportunities you presented in the vision play, you have everyone's attention and they are now eager to hear what strategic options and responses you have to propose.

Now you actually have to come up with a set of thoughtful strategic responses to the issues you uncovered in the vision play. But the good news is you don't need to do it all alone. You will of course work the nemawashi process with the strategy play in the same way you did with the vision play. However, unlike with the vision play, with the strategy play you need to get back to the forum you assembled pretty quickly so you don't lose momentum.

As you prepare for the strategy play, it is once again critical that you realize what your objectives are. Let's start with what they are not: It is not your objective to present your full and complete IT strategy. That would be a big mistake at this point. (If all goes well, you will have that opportunity later.)

You have just gotten into the key strategic decision-making forum and as such you have one key objective: To secure your attendance and participation in this forum long term. That means you need to: (a) reinforce the importance and value of your input, and (b) carve out a clear and logical role for yourself going forward.

Given these objectives, it should make sense to you that the key questions you need to answer in the strategy play presentation are:

1. Given all that you know about technology, your industry, your customers, and your competitors, what are the company's best options for response?

2. How might you apply technological and other solutions to the issues you identified?

3. What options are there to capitalize on the opportunities identified in your vision?

4. What key initiatives should be undertaken to turn these ideas into action?

5. What are the potential outcomes from the various moves?

6. What will they cost and what benefit might they bring?

Strategic options work best

It is my very strongest recommendation that you present a set of options for response to the challenges and opportunities. When you present one option for review and approval, you invite challenge and rejection. However, when you present options, people join you in determining the final answer.

Now with a set of options to choose from, you and the executive leadership can engage in a final discussion to determine what will be done. Of course, as would only be proper for the IT leader who has brought these issues to the forefront of the company's awareness, you will "volunteer" to oversee (along with a business colleague) any of the IT-based initiatives directed at addressing the identified challenges and opportunities.

Once those choices are made, you are on your way. You are now part of the team that is overseeing the implementation of the company's most strategic initiatives. In conjunction with your business colleague(s), you will be returning to meet with this committee in order to provide updates and progress reports.

Congratulations!

You have your seat at the table. Not because someone gave it to you. But because you put yourself there. You gave it to yourself by virtue of the value you have added to the company beginning back with *Secret #1* and working your way up to the key strategy forum of the company.

The question of course now is: what happens next? Will you be invited back to the forum meetings only when your area and initiatives are up for discussion, or will you become a de facto permanent member of this group? Will your newly "strategic" profile lead to greater responsibilities? Greater compensation? Greater influence in other areas?

The answer to what happens next is of course dependent on how well you execute on your strategic initiatives and on your continued adherence to Secrets 1–9. But there are two other critical elements to your influence and success that really kick in now that you are at this level. We'll uncover them in *Secrets #10* and *#11*, coming up.

GET YOUR TEAM TO REALLY PLAY

"Wars may be fought with weapons, but they are won by man. It is the spirit of the men who follow and of the man who leads that gain the victory."

General George Smith Patton

You can't do it all alone

While a few of *The Secrets* we have covered thus far focus specifically on your personal behavior and actions, the overwhelming majority of *The Secrets* cannot be put to work without the help and support of your team. This presents you with a pretty important challenge: How do you get your people behind you to support this influence-building agenda? Specifically, How do you:

- Ensure that the infrastructure group follows through on your increased demands for service?

- Get assistance doing the research and prep work required to fully understand the business?

- Implement tighter reporting around budgets and costs without feeling like you are breathing down their neck?

- Enlist the support of your senior staff to fashion a compelling vision and strategy?

It's not enough to just have your team following your new agenda and doing the specific things you ask of them, you want them to be "into it." You want—actually, it's probably more correct to say—you need your team to be fully behind you on this initiative. No simple feat.

If you're like most IT leaders, you're probably remembering the last performance improvement initiative you took on, or maybe even the one or two before that; and how well those ended up. Not because the initiatives themselves were such bad ideas, but because it was just so hard to motivate your team to implement them. They were always just so busy with other important work that it never really made sense to push them on the changes you wanted made. (Well, at least it feels good to say that's the reason.) At any rate, despite the best intentions, the change never came to life. It was just too hard to motivate your team into sustained action.

So what's going to be different this time? What are you going to do to get your people behind you on this one? That's the focus of this chapter. In other words, what is the secret to really getting your team behind you on change initiatives? What special things, if any, do highly influential IT leaders do in order to motivate their teams and to secure their support for implementing the changes required to build influence.

Why I care

This is a topic that is very dear to my heart, because I've been a bit of a punching bag on this issue myself.

I'll explain: As a consultant I am often hired by the CIO or similar level of the company. I spend a lot of time listening to my new client and learning about their special requirements and needs. Together, we work through an approach to the project. But then the time comes to assemble the data and information, in other words—the real work. That's when I have to go to work with the next one or two levels down. And let me tell you, most of the time, they are not too happy to see me. Because even though their boss may want me to help do something, these guys are far from bought in on the idea.

That's why I typically spend the first 20%-30% of my time for any given assignment explaining the initiative and building support for it with the IT leader's team. Forget that it's sometimes a very emotionally trying process for me; it's expensive and time consuming for the client. But, this isn't always the case. In a minority of situations I'll encounter a team that is either pretty well briefed on the initiative or one that is very open and eager to "give it a shot"—so to speak.

I started to pay close attention to what was different about the "give it a shot" crowd and their IT leader, versus all the other groups I dealt with. What was it that seemed to motivate one group over the other? What was common to the "give it a shot" crowd, even if they differed in many other ways, that made them supportive of their bosses' change programs?

I was interested in learning what could be done to motivate teams to support change initiatives (like the ones I was driving) without a ton of time-consuming selling and establishing "buy in" activity.

I carefully observed different client teams and the management styles of their leaders. And for a long period of time, I asked nearly every IT professional I worked with a few simple questions:

- What is it you most want to see in your boss?

- What is it you most want your boss to do for you?

- What can your boss do to get you to support this change initiative? (Whatever it happened to be at the time)

- What has any IT leader, for whom you have worked in the past, done that has been particularly instrumental in influencing you to support their agenda?

What I learned

Of all the possible things that an IT leader can do to create a positive atmosphere and to motivate their staff to support change initiatives, there are three things that matter the most. Of the hundreds of possible tactics an IT leader can employ, these three items were consistently ranked as most important for driving motivation. More important than changes in title, instituting bonuses, or even receiving raises. These three items mattered the most for building motivation and support for change.

When these items, these "motivators," are present, IT leaders are able to count on a much greater degree of support and flexibility from their teams. It's the secret of getting your team to really play. They are:

1. The presence of a clear vision and strategy

2. A proactive approach to change

3. Tangible investments in external professional development

1. The presence of a clear vision and strategy

Universally—and I mean across all industries and all levels of the organization—IT professionals and managers say that they are motivated by seeing a real vision. They want to see that their leader knows where the group should be going and has a plan for getting there.

This is more than just having a nice presentation. They want to see that the vision and strategy is being communicated and is understood by the broader user community. They want to know that the business understands and is behind the vision and strategy articulated by IT. More than that, they want to know how their work fits into the vision and they want to feel actively part of the bigger picture and plan.

Then, when they see how what they are being asked to do fits into the vision, they are happy to go along with the program. In fact, they welcome taking concrete action on the vision. They may not always articulate it quite this way, but when you talk to them, a clear sense of vision is what they crave and respect.

When you follow the script for *Your Three Signature Plays*, you initiate a nemawashi process with your own team around all aspects of IT vision and strategy. Then, from the output of these discussions with your own team, you are able to take the first steps toward your business colleagues, peers, customers, stakeholders and boss.

The process of including them in every key step of the process and jointly building the materials to support *Your Three Signature Plays*, will actively demonstrate your vision in just the manner IT professionals desire to see.

Here's the best part. If you think having a tight vision presentation impresses your senior leadership, wait until you see the impact if will have on your own team. When you do that big IT vision presentation for your group at an upcoming company event, they are going to be brimming with pride at what they feel is very much theirs.

All really good reasons to get on this right away.

2. A proactive approach to change

IT professionals and managers, like most knowledge workers these days, are forever in the throws of change. Whether due to new project assignments, mergers and acquisitions, outsourcing, rightsizing, or just plain old internal reorganization, the roles and responsibilities of IT folk are frequently subject to change. It's therefore not all that surprising that an important factor in determining their level of openness to change and willingness to support a new agenda was how the CIO managed change on their behalf.

Highly motivated team members frequently described their IT leader's handling of change as "proactive." They often spoke of how their boss was always highly attuned to possible changes to roles and responsibilities anywhere in the organization and the possible ripple through to the IT group. In fact, some look for change opportunities.

Because when organizational shifts arise, they use them to actively advance their people's careers forward. They try to move their people around the IT organization in order to broaden their experience. They also work to get them experience in areas outside of IT.

Another important facet to "a proactive approach to change" is how much time IT leaders spend on the change after it has been officially rolled out. What I have found—as a general rule—is that the really influential IT leaders, the ones with the best rapport with their staff and who enjoy the highest degree of motivation from their team, are spending up to 50% of their time shepherding change in close contact with their people. That is very different from how most IT leaders manage.

The more common approach to change is minimalist; where IT leaders pay little mindful attention to organizational changes. They allocate time and effort to change management only as much as they absolutely have to as required by HR, or to get people working productively. And of course, all the "soft" aspects of role and personnel change management are particularly unpopular management activities for most IT leaders.

In the end however, this turns out to be very important for building a motivated and open-minded team.

3. Tangible investments in external professional development

The first two motivators have a lot to do with how the IT leader manages in two key dimensions and the kind of atmosphere and environment that is created as a result. The last motivator is much more personal. It is a clear expression of what IT professionals want and value: professional development. And in particular, external professional development.

IT professionals and managers are more committed to, and more motivated to work for, leaders that invest in their professional development. They place particular importance on attending conferences, business and industry workshops, and technical training programs. In addition to the CBTs and internal resources, IT professionals and managers place a great deal of value on external encounters. They also want support to develop strategic competencies like facilitation, presentation delivery, and business analysis.

This is perhaps the most crucial point in this entire chapter, because it is also the easiest item to implement immediately. More importantly, it brings near immediate returns. Almost as soon as you announce and make available new and exciting external professional development, you enjoy a halo effect with your team.

What does this means for you? It means that if you want to build the motivation of your team to get behind your agenda, influence-building or otherwise, increase your investment in professional development. But not just your financial investment, your time and energy as well. Spend time learning what kind of professional development is important to your people and make it a priority to help them achieve it.

What's so special about these three items?

I can't say for sure what it is about these three things that has such a strong effect on IT people, but they do. Sales people would likely have put money high up on their motivating factors list, but that isn't what's critical to IT folks—at least not in this context. It is these three actions (or sets of actions) that contribute to creating an environment where IT professionals and managers comfortably rally behind their bosses' change initiatives with an open mind and positive attitude. And since your goal is to get your team on your side and executing with you, knowing what's really important to your people can be incredibly helpful. Of course the real value only comes when you act on it.

Concluding story

The story that best illustrates this point comes from two people whose names I never knew (you'll see why in a moment). I'll call them Todd and Andrew to make it easier for me to tell the story.

It happened when I was speaking at a conference. As often happens after a talk, people came up to continue the conversation. I was just getting ready to talk to the last person waiting (Todd) when another person (Andrew) walked up.

A look of instant recognition passed between them and they began to exclaim about how long it had been since they had worked together, ask about each other, and catch up. They caught themselves and returned to question me, but I encouraged them to go ahead and catch up, while I "eavesdropped" on their exchange.

I can't remember exactly what they said, but the gist of it was this:

Todd: What a coincidence. What are you doing here? What are you doing now?

Andrew: I'm an Executive Director of Business Intelligence. I look after a group of 40 people supporting our clinical research multi-terabyte data warehouse.

Todd: Wow, that's a big job. How did you land it?

Andrew: Honestly, as much as I'd like to take the credit, it wasn't really me. When I left the company we were at, and landed at my current place we were a mid-size team, maybe 100 in IT overall. But over the next few years we went through a couple of mergers and acquisitions and our group grew pretty substantially. Along the way our CIO seemed to always end up on top, somehow she just kept up. And she kept me up as well.

Every so often I was given opportunities to try new stuff. She was always moving me around, encouraging me to try new things, to move out into the business; that's how I got involved with the clinical group.

When this job came up, even though it is out of her group, she encouraged me to go for it. And when I applied for it, I realized I'd worked in pretty much every area they needed experience with. All that moving around and staying up on the latest changes really paid off. I don't think that would have happened if she hadn't been looking out for me for a long time.

So … what do you think your team will say about you at the next conference they attend?

SECRET #11

TAKE YOUR GAME ON THE ROAD

"It's clear that I am being granted abroad the recognition and affection I was denied at home."

Acclaimed Spanish filmmaker, Pedro Almodovar
After winning the Oscar for "All About My Mother"

Again…it's not what you think

We've come to the last secret. Like many of the earlier secrets, the essence of this secret is found in the subtle differences between conventional wisdom and the special understandings and practices of the highly influential IT leaders.

On the surface, the phrase *Take Your Game on the Road* conjures up images of self-promotion and marketing. And that's not surprising. There are certainly many articles, books and seminars that call upon (and attempt to teach) IT leaders to better market themselves.

This approach urges IT leaders to adopt a full frontal assault, to "get out there" and do presentations on "the business value of IT." And so, using a wide variety of methods and supported by a host of PowerPoint-induced contortions, IT leaders attempt to show the connection between IT activities and the latest increase in sales—usually with very little success.

There are however two big mistakes with this approach to *Take Your Game on the Road*: (1) It shifts the emphasis to marketing and off of crisp performance, and (2) the focus tends to be internal in nature.

It's not that I am against communicating the value of IT; quite the contrary, I am a huge believer in it. It's just that I have found that the very best way to demonstrate the value of IT is to have people experience it in a very tangible way —not to be told about it.

Additionally, the internally-oriented approach to *Take Your Game on the Road* has resulted in the over-branding of IT. Eager to operationalize the marketing ideas they hear of in the popular press, IT groups all over the world are now creating their own logos and cute little tag lines, many of which change with every shift in strategy. But this notion of a separate brand within the company only reinforces the message that IT is not a part of the business, and that you are not like everyone else. Can you imagine the finance or sales group doing something like this?

This same misunderstanding of branding has carried through to even the best intentioned IT leaders. Eager to build their personal brands, many CIOs have taken upon themselves a number of activities they believe will increase their profile and the profile of the IT group as a whole. But as reported by Harvey Nash in their 2008 study on the topic, the lion's share of their efforts are focused on less than compelling brand-building activities. Here, for example, were the top three activities reported by CIOs as part of their personal brand-building efforts.

1. I regularly go out of my way to be physically seen in the business.

2. I always ensure that personal information on social websites (such as LinkedIn) is kept accurate and up to date.

3. I ensure my name is on all relevant emails/communications that go out from the IT department to the business.

It's not that these activities are bad or wrong per se. It's just that face time, LinkedIn, and email aren't going to generate a whole lot of respect and influence with your executive leadership.

So what is it then?

It's really just one very slight shift that makes all the difference. *Take Your Game on the Road* means to say that in order for you to maximize your influence and respect at home, you need to establish a respected presence away from home.

To be held in high regard within your company you need to be held in high regard outside of your company. Practically, this means that you need to establish a reputation for yourself and your team outside of the walls of your own company. You and your team need to be seen on the playing field of your industry and beyond.

Now, I can just imagine what you might be thinking at this moment:

Hold on Marc. All along you have told me that these secrets are not about ruthless self-promotion and political manipulation. And now you are telling me that in order to reach the pinnacle of influence in my own company, I have to go out and impress a bunch of strangers. What gives?

I understand why that would be your first reaction. At first read it seems just that way. And that is exactly why this is largely a secret, and practiced only by a very few IT leaders. But the truth is that I am not going to ask you to engage in a personal crusade to "impress a bunch of strangers." Rather, I am going to challenge you to do what the most influential IT leaders have challenged themselves to do over the years, and that is:

- To become a full-fledged member of the greater IT community
- To put yourself "out there" and to be open to criticism so that you can improve
- To share your very best practices with your colleagues just as you wish them to share with you
- To learn by teaching others
- To provide opportunities for personal satisfaction for your team
- To build a network of colleagues upon whom you can rely when you're in a pinch

And that is what *Take Your Game on the Road* is really all about.

What does that have to do with influence?

When you *Take Your Game on the Road* in this manner, you get noticed—you stand out. You start to become a respected figure within your industry and beyond. You get quoted in periodicals. Your team's showcase projects win industry awards and are written about in the major trade journals. You start to become a requested speaker at industry events. You are invited to sit on vendor advisory boards. Headhunters start to call.

As all this is happening—almost by magic (OK, maybe not completely by magic)—your colleagues, peers and bosses start to learn of your reputation outside of the company. And like a slightly took-you-for-granted, possessive spouse they start to see that others find you very attractive. And with a mixture of pride and a touch of anxious jealousy, they start to really see you for who you are and begin to accord you the full respect and influence you now deserve.

Why is this the case?

Simple. Because to some extent—no matter how well you deliver on *Secrets #1-#10* —your colleagues will still see you as the "IT guy." Even though they now sit with you in the strategy meetings, they still experience you as the guy who keeps the systems running, handles the budgets for tech support and oversees application development. You know, all that tech stuff. And people being people, perceptions change slowly and usually only when they are "helped" along. It's just human nature.

When you and your team start to receive external respect and validation, it resets the opinion and perception of your own internal colleagues. In a largely subconscious way they say to themselves, "if all these other people respect and admire my CIO, then he must really be something special."

A related phenomenon, familiar to every CIO, is the way external consultants can take a position and instantly be believed, whereas if the CIO were to use the exact same words, his view might be discounted—What gives?

Again, it's human nature: familiarity breeds contempt. You are seen as coming from within, being part of the organization. The consultants, by contrast, are assumed to have garnered their experiences, gleaned their insights, and developed their reputations from work outside your company—which, in the eyes of most, instantly and magically bestows respect.

What this secret highlights is the fact that sometimes the best way to convince your colleagues of your value is not to try and convince them at all. Instead, the better approach is to allow them to be convinced by others. And that's how you break through the structural limitations to your influence that come from being an insider.

It ain't just theory

Let's make it real by taking a look at a number of IT leaders (some of whom you have already met earlier in this book) who are making this journey.

- **Kumud Kalia,** CIO - Direct Energy has been named "best in class" and among the 100 Premier IT Leaders by Computerworld magazine. Under Kalia's leadership Direct Energy was identified as "one of the 100 best places to work in IT." He is a fellow of both the British Computer Society and the Institution of Engineering & Technology. He is also a contributing author to the CIO IT Leadership network.

- **Brian Lurie,** CIO - Stryker Orthopedics was named by Computerworld as a Premier 100 IT Leader and has received the Top 10 Leaders & Innovators Award from the Global CIO Executive Summit. Lurie is a charter member of Temple University Computer and Information Sciences Advisory, serves on the panel of Global Technology Confidence Indicators (GTCI) for the Stevens Technology Institute and is a frequent industry speaker.

- **Stephen Squeri,** CIO - American Express Company also serves as group president of Global Services. Squeri has been an Independent Director of The Guardian Life Insurance Company of America since 2009. He is also a Member of the Board of Trustees of New York Downtown and Harlem Children's Zone, and a member of the Board of Governors of Monsignor McClancy Memorial High School.

- **Glen Salow,** EVP Service Delivery & Technology - Ameriprise Financial Inc. He serves on the New York Presbyterian Technology Advisory Board, the British Petroleum Technology Advisory Board, the IBM Customer Advisory Board, and the Avaya Customer Advisory Board. He is also a member of the CIO Strategy Exchange.

Impressive, isn't it.

Getting on to the road

If taking your game on the road is not about shameless self-promotion (which usually isn't all that effective anyway) and instead is about contribution, fellowship and leadership, how do you get started? What do you do first?

The truth is it really doesn't matter where you get started as long as you do. No one just bursts on to the scene and immediately seizes a spot at the top. It takes time, a long-term commitment, and a genuine desire to contribute to the community. Opportunities vary and different IT leaders go about it in different ways. Here are a few ways to get started.

- Answer "calls for papers" that are put out by a variety of conferences.
- Enter a few of your showcase projects in the awards competitions run by software vendors, publications and industry groups. (This is a favorite of mine because it provides an opportunity for your team to shine.)
- Participate in industry forums and round tables.
- Contribute to best practice databases.
- Make friends with the professional press. For example: offer your favorite industry journalists an opportunity to ask questions about how you do things.
- Volunteer to serve on the IT advisory board of your local hospital or other similar not-for-profit institution.
- Write an article for an industry publication or website.
- Write a blog.
- Sponsor a peer breakfast meeting at your company on your favorite topic.

But don't forget the essence of the secret

As you move forward with this secret, I encourage you to remember that although you are likely to enjoy influence benefits down the road, this isn't how you should approach it from the start. Stay focused on the intrinsic merits of what you are doing; the internal influence piece will take care of itself in the right time. A few examples of this attitude to encourage you on this path:

Nick Lansley is the head of R&D of Tesco.com. In 2010 Nick was named by Wired UK as a member of the "Wired 100" and one of Britain's top digital power brokers. But back in October 2008 when he was first launching his "Technology for Tesco" blog he didn't set big-time recognition as his goal. Rather, he wrote that the purpose of his blog was to "let you know about the technology research projects I am working on, the people I am meeting to get these projects up and running, and how and why I have chosen them."

Notice the open and inquiring attitude Nick brought to the endeavor. It's not easy to put yourself out there and to invite comments, but when you are serious about sharing and learning, this is what you do. It's no wonder how things have turned out for him.

Another noteworthy UK-based CIO is Peter Birley of law firm Browne Jacobson. In 2009 Peter was voted one of the UK's most influential and innovative CIOs with additional recognitions in 2010 as well. Peter also established a blog in order to: "share thoughts, issues and concerns with the management of IT and hopefully (if anybody reads it) to get some feedback and discussion that is helpful to all."

And finally there is Linda Cureton, the CIO for NASA. It's a big job with a great deal of responsibility, but she approaches it with a sense of humility and openness. How do I know? Not because I have ever done any work for NASA, but because I read her blog. In one particularly revealing entry she reflects on why she blogs and says:

> "I am not comfortable and I am afraid. So, why do I blog? Here are my reasons:
>
> - To learn and demonstrate the value of Web 2.0 technologies supporting the spirit of innovation that should be required of the NASA CIO
>
> - To communicate to stakeholders and customers the activities and issues
>
> - To focus my thoughts and learnings to the things that matter in my role as CIO
>
> - To increase my leadership abilities to those I serve by providing a means for them to get to know the real me."

Once you get started on this path, you will be surprised how quickly you begin to see benefits. From interacting with your peers you will learn a lot about what's going on outside of your company which will be very valuable to your vision and strategy development work. What's more, peer interaction will challenge you to put your best foot forward. The result: your game will improve and you will feel really good about yourself for having made the stretch.

But it doesn't end there. Your expanding knowledge, network and reputation will further solidify your leadership position with your staff and will make recruiting much easier.

All in all, *Take Your Game on the Road* is a great thing to do for your professional development and the professional development of your team. And by the way, it also happens to be a great catalyst to enhancing your influence and position with your colleagues, peers, customers, stakeholders, and boss.

CONCLUSION

When we first set out on this journey together, you may have been a little unsure about the pursuit of influence. You may have felt that there was an insurmountable barrier between you and influence. Perhaps you believed that achieving meaningful influence was out of your reach—available only to those who have the right personality or some set of near-magical skills.

Over the last 11 chapters we have systematically dismantled that barrier; taking it down piece by piece. In its place, we have constructed a road to influence with each of *The Secrets* providing guidance, support and provisions for the journey. Because it turns out that the road to influence, while sometimes challenging to travel, is made up nothing more than a set of simple, practical and doable steps that, when followed, lead you straight to the executive suite.

I uncovered and developed *The Secrets* over 20+ years of working with, consulting to, and mentoring IT leaders and their teams all over the world. Now that I have shared *The Secrets* with you, it's my hope (and expectation) that you are already putting them to work and making them your own.

So, what's next?

Actually, I have something to ask of you. I want to ask you to pay it forward.

What does that mean? It means I want you to do more than just improve your personal influence and professional success. I want you to join me and help improve the state of leadership and influence for IT professionals all over the world. How? First of all, share *The Secrets*; and share what they are doing for you. Help your peers, team members, employees—anyone you interact with professionally—to do better with these tools.

Second, to all those pundits claiming the end of the IT leader is near, join me and emphatically say it ain't so. The next time you attend a conference where people are lamenting the imminent demise of the CIO, step up and say it doesn't have to be that way. When you read an article or blog post that echos with "oh me, oh my," comment on it, take a stand. Use what you've learned to take the conversation in a more positive, forward-thinking direction. (By the way, this won't hurt your take-it-on-the-road efforts either.)

And finally, contribute to the discussion and the advancement of these ideas. If you enjoy a particular success, uncover a new aspect to *The Secrets*, or perhaps develop a new one altogether, email me or share it on my blog (http://marcjschiller.com/blog). Together we will create a community of IT leaders dedicated to the very best things that influence can bring and we'll help change the game of IT leadership and management for the better—for everyone.

Until our next conversation,

Marc J. Schiller

mjs@marcjschiller.com

REFERENCES

Books

Austin, Richard D., Nolan, Richard L., and O'Donnell, Shannon. *The Adventures of an IT Leader.* Boston: Harvard Business Press, 2009.

Broadbent, Marianne, and Kitzis, Ellen S. *The New CIO Leader, Setting the Agenda and Delivering.* Boston: Harvard Business Press, 2004.

Carnegie, Dale. *How to Win Friends and Influence People.* New York: Pocket, 1982.

Carr, Nicholas G. *Does IT Matter? Information Technology and the Corrosion of Competitive Advantage.* Boston: Harvard Business Press, 2004.

Cialdidi, Robert B. *Influence Science and Practice.* Upper Saddle River: Prentice Hall, 2008.

Cooper, Alan. *About Face.* Foster City: IDG Books Worldwide, Inc., 1995

Edwards, Mickey, Thakrar, Usha, and Watkins, Michael. *Winning the Influence Game: What Every Business Leader Should Know about Government.* Hoboken: Wiley, 2001.

Fetherling, Dale, and Witt, Christopher. *Real Leaders Don't Do Powerpoint, How to Sell Yourself and Your Idea.* New York: Crown Business, 2009.

Fingar, Peter, and Smith, Howard. *IT Doesn't Matter Business Processes Do.* Tampa: Meghan Kiffer Press, 2003.

Gardner, Christopher. *The Valuation of Information Technology.* New York: John Wiley & Sons, Inc., 2000.

Goldratt, Eliyahu M. and Cox, Jeff. *The Goal.* New Haven: North River Press, Inc., 2004

Goleman, Daniel. *Emotional Intelligence: Why It Can Matter More Than IQ.* New York: Bantam, 1997.

Hogan, Kevin. *The Science of Influence: How to get Anyone to say YES in 8 Minutes or Less.* Hoboken: Wiley, 2004.

Hunter, Richard, and Westerman, George. *The Real Business of IT: How CIOs Create and Communicate Value.* Boston: Harvard Business Press, 2009.

Krause, Donald G. *The Art of War For Executives: Ancient Knowledge for Today's Business Professional.* New York: Perigree Trade, 1995.

Lane, Dean. *CIO Wisdom: Best Practices from Silicon Valley's Leading IT Experts.* Upper Saddle River: Prentice Hall, 2003.

Lieberman, David J. *Get Anyone to Do Anything.* New York: St. Martin's Griffin, 2001.

Maguire, Steve. *Debugging The Development Process.* Redmond: Microsoft Press 1994.

McCormack, Ade. *The IT Value Stack: A Boardroom Guide to IT Leadership.* Hoboken: Wiley, 2008.

Minoli, Daniel. *Analyzing Outsourcing.* McGraw-Hill, Inc, 1994.

Mortenson, Kurt W. *Maximum Influence: The 12 Universal Laws of Power Persuasion.* New York: AMACOM, 2004.

Palmer, Stephanie. *Good in a Room.* Doubleday, 2008.

Watkins, Michael. *The First 90 Days: Critical Success Strategies for New Leaders at All Levels.* Boston: Harvard Business Press, 2003.

Articles and essays

Baker, Pam. "IT Leadership; Building a Business Case to Save Your Job." *CIO Update* 10 Jun. 2010.

Betts, Mitch. "Book Review: Four Steps to Becoming a Top-Tier CIO." *CIO* 16 Nov. 2009.

Broadbent, M., McGee, K., McDonald, M. "IT Success Requires Discipline and Innovation." *Gartner* 12 May 2003.

Bulkeley, William M. "CIOs Boost Their Profile as They Become Cost Cutters." *Wall Street Journal* 11 Mar. 2003.

CIO UK Staff. "Innovative CIOs Gain Strategic Influence." *CIO* 15 May 2008.

Craig David, Tinaikar Ranjit. "Divide and Conquer: Rethinking IT Strategy." *McKinsey Quarterly* Aug 2006.

Dajani, Mark Senior VP and CIO, Kraft Foods. "CIO Profiles." *InformationWeek* 21 November 2009.

DeLisi, Peter, Moberg, Dennis, Danielson, Ronald. "Why CIO's Are Last Among Equals." *MIT Sloan Management* Review 20 May 2010.

Dempsey, Jed, Dvorak, Robert E., Holen, Endre, Mark, David, Meehan, William F. III. "A Hard and Soft Look at IT Investments." *McKinsey Quarterly* Feb 1998.

Enns, Harvey G. Huff, Sid L. Golden, Brian R. "CIO Influence Behaviors: The Impact of Technical Backgroup." *Information and Management.* May 2003.

Enns, Harvey G. Huff, Sid L. Higgins, Christopher A. "CIO Lateral Influence Behaviors: Gaining Peers' Commitment to Strategic Information Systems." *Management Information Systems Research Center, University of Minnesota.* March 2003.

Evans, Bob. "Business Technology: IT Is A Must, No Matter How You View It." *InformationWeek* 23 May 2003.

Evans, Bob. "Do CIOs Still Matter?" *InformationWeek* 8 Feb. 2010.

Flanagan, Thomas Senior VP and CIO, Amgen. Hofman, Michel Head of Systems and Development Europe, Rabobank International. Carmondy, Cora Senior VP of IT Jacobs Engineering. "Building Your Power Base — Credibility and Strong Relationships Establish CIO Influence with Stakeholders." *CIO* 1 April 2010.

Gandossy, Robert, Guarnieri, Robin. *"Can You Measure Leadership?"* MIT Sloan Management Review 1 Oct. 2008.

Gillooly, Brian. "CIOs Gain Influence And Responsibility." *Information Week* 4 June 2007

Gray, Patrick. "The Split Personality CIO." *Tech Republic* 1 Jun. 2010.

Grenney, Joseph, and McMillan, Ron. "The Influencers: The Top Five Reasons Leaders Lack Influence." *Training* 17 Nov. 2008.

Grenny, Joseph, Maxfield, David, Shimberg, Andrew. "How to Have Influence." *MIT Sloan Management Review* 1 Oct. 2008.

Gruman, Galen. "How to Communicate ROI to the Business." *CIO* 8 Oct. 2007.

Heller, Martha. "Battling Lack of IT Understanding." *CIO* 23 Feb. 2010.

Heller, Martha. "Stop Educating the Business and Start Delivering Value." *CIO* 27 Aug. 2010.

Hill, Linda A. "What it Really Means to Manage: Exercising Power and Influence." *Harvard Business Press* 11 Aug. 1999.

Hill, Linda A., Lineback, Kent. "Can People Trust You?: Influence Begins with Trust—Why Earning the Trust of Others is Key to Becoming a Great Boss." *Harvard Business Press* 11 Jan. 2011.

Hill, Linda A., Lineback, Kent. "Understand the Reality of Your Organization: You Need Influence to Make Your Team Effective—Why Engaging the Larger Organization is Imperative to Becoming a Great Boss." *Harvard Business Press* 11 Jan. 2011.

Javitch, David. "Grow Your Power, Boost Your Influence." *Entrepreneur* 23 Feb. 2009.

Keefe, P. "IT Does Matter." *ComputerWorld* 12 May 2003.

Laartz, Jurgen, Monnoyer, Eric, Scherdin, Alexander. "Designing IT For Business." *McKinsey Quarterly* Aug 2003.

Levinson, Meredith. "Project Management: How IT and Business Relationships Shape Success." *CIO* 16 Sept. 2009.

Lohmeyer, Dan, Pogreb, Sofya, Robinson, Scott. "Who's Accountable for IT?" *McKinsey Quarterly* Dec. 2002.

Long Lingo, Elizabeth, McGinn, Kathleen L. "Power and Influence: Achieving Your Objectives in Organizations." *Harvard Business Press* 21 Mar. 2001.

Magretta, Joan, Stone, Nate. "What Management Is: How it Works and Why." *New York: Free Press* 2002.

Malone, Thomas W. "The Future of Work: How the New Order of Business Will Shape Your Organization, Your Management Style and Your Life." *Harvard Business Press* 2004.

Mark, David, Monnoyer, Eric. "Next-Generation CIOs." *McKinsey Quarterly* Jul. 2004.

Mattern, Frank, Schonwalder, Stephan, Stein, Wolfram. "Fighting Complexity in IT." *McKinsey Quarterly* Feb. 2003.

McKee, John. "3 Proven Tips for IT Leaders." *Tech Republic* 19 Feb. 2009.

McKenna, Michelle. "Think Like Your Customer." *CIO* 1 July 2008.

Melymuka, K. "IT Does So Matter!" *ComputerWorld* 7 Jul. 2003.

Mendi, Murat A. "Proving IT's Value to the Business." *CIO Update* 9 Sept. 2010.

Monnoyer, Eric, Willmott, Paul. "What IT Leaders Do." *McKinsey Quarterly* Aug 2005.

Mulholland, Andy. "Model The Power to Influence. The new generation of CIO's: Walk in the Shoes' of the Leaders that Drive Change and Business Growth!" *Capgemini* 18 Aug. 2008.

Nash, Kim. "The Top Line Interview: Betsy Burton." *CIO* 11 Nov. 2009.

Nolan, Richard, McFarlan, Warren F. "Information Technology and the Board of Directors." *Harvard Business Review* Oct. 2005.

Schrage, Michael. "Wal-Mart Trumps Moore's Law." *Technology Review* Mar. 2002.

Soat, John. "CIO Influence is Waning." *Wall Street and Technology* December 2007.

Taschek, John. "IT Does Matter." *eWeek* 14 Jul. 2003.

Wailgum, Thomas. "Why CFOs and CEOs Hate IT." *CIO* 8 Apr. 2009.

Wang, Yunfeng. Chen, Xiaochun. Zhao, Zhao. "The Integrative Model of CIO Lateral Influence Behavior, Peer's Trust and Peer's Commitment." *IEEE Computer Society* 2008

Watkins, Michael. "Winning the Influence Game: Corporate Diplomacy and Business Strategy." *Harvard Business Press* 22 Apr. 2003.

Westerman, G. and Weill, P. "What Makes CIOs Effective: The Perspective of Non-IT Executives." *MIT Sloan CISR Research Briefings* Jul. 2005.

Whitting, R. "CIOs Sure Think IT Matters." *Information Week* 23 May 2003.

Surveys and reports

Capgemini Consulting. "The Role of the IT Function in Business Innovation – Operator vs. Innovator." 2008.

Gartner Executive Programs Premier Report. "Making the Difference: The 2008 CIO Agenda." Jan. 2008.

Harvey Nash and CIO UK. "CIO Personal Branding." September 2008.

Websites and blogs

http://advice.cio.com

http://www.bio-itworld.com

http://blogs.nasa.gov/cm/newui/blog/viewpostlist.jsp?blogname=NASA-CIO-Blog

http://blogs.wsj.com/biztech/

http://www.cio.com

http://www.cioblog.co.uk

http://www.cioindex.com

http://www.cioinsight.com

http://www.cioupdate.com

http://www.itstrategycenter.com

http://www.computerworld.com

http://www.dama.org

http://www.eweek.com

http://www.fiercecio.com

http://www.fiercehealthit.com

http://www.govtech.com

http://www.govtech.com/blogs/index

http://www.healthdatamanagement.com

http://www.information-management.com

http://www.informationweek.com

http://www.infoworld.com

http://www.itworld.com

http://www.itworldcanada.com

http://techfortesco.blogspot.com/

http://www.techrepublic.com

http://totalcio.blogs.techtarget.com